from Idea to Matter

Curated by Edward Albee

Nine Sculptors

John Beech

John Duff

David Fulton

Barry Goldberg

David McDonald

Richard Nonas

Jonathan Thomas

Mia Westerlund Roosen

Paul Whiting

This catalogue was published in conjunction with the exhibition *From Idea to Matter: Nine Sculptors*
Curated by Edward Albee

October 20 – December 17, 2000
Anderson Gallery
Virginia Commonwealth University
School of the Arts

Designer: Laura Chessin

Editor: George Cruger

Publication Coordinator: Amy G. Moorefield

Printer: Worth Higgins, Richmond, VA

Distributed by the
University of Washington Press
P.O. Box 50096
Seattle, WA 98145-5096

Copyright © October 2000
Published by Anderson Gallery,
Virginia Commonwealth University
School of the Arts
907 1/2 West Franklin Street
Richmond, VA 23284-2514
ph. 804.828.1522
fax. 804.828.8585
www.vcu.edu/artweb/gallery

"Context is All: Notes and Conversations"
Copyright © 2000 Edward Albee and Harry Rand

"From Idea To Matter: Some Thoughts on Sculpture"
Copyright © 2000 Edward Albee

" What Matters"
Copyright © 2000, Harry Rand

Works are courtesy of the artists, with the exception
of eight works on loan from the curator's collection.

Library of Congress Card Number: 00-108632
ISBN 0-935519-23-8

Nine Sculptors

Anderson Gallery

Virginia Commonwealth University

School of the Arts

Richmond, Virginia

October 20 – December 17, 2000

Nine Sculptors

Anderson Gallery

Virginia Commonwealth University

School of the Arts

Richmond, Virginia

October 20 – December 17, 2000

Contents

5   **Foreword**
by Ted Potter

7   **Introduction**
From Idea to Matter: Some Thoughts on Sculpture
by Edward Albee

9-29   ***Context is All:***
Notes and Conversations
with Edward Albee and Harry Rand

31-41   ***What Matters***
by Harry Rand

42-59   **Artists' Biographies**

60-61   **Checklist**

Be wary, however, of letting him into your studio;

for he will surely instruct you concerning which

of your paintings are finished and which are not …

Foreword

Ted Potter, *Director*
Anderson Gallery

Virginia
Commonwealth
University

School of the Arts

Over the twenty some years I've known Edward Albee, I have learned almost as much about the visual arts as I did in both under-graduate and graduate school. Be wary, however, of letting him into your studio; for he will surely instruct you concerning which of your paintings are finished and which are not — and that it's about time you stopped attempting to paint like Gorky (who has been dead now fifty years or more). The above is merely noted as but one example, among many, as to why I was interested in having him curate the collection of works from nine artists he selected for this exhibition, *From Idea to Matter*. I have developed a strong professional respect for and trust in his ability to know " Real Art" when he sees it. In this collection of sculpture, Albee has demonstrated his strong interest in the raw, weathered surface of the (hands on) human encounter.

The Anderson Gallery of Virginia Commonwealth University's School of the Arts is honored to present the work of the nine outstanding sculptors Mr. Albee has curated for this show. Without exception their work is strong, confident and intelligent. The Anderson Gallery is indebted to the artists in *From Idea to Matter:* John Beech, John Duff, David Fulton, Barry Goldberg, David McDonald, Richard Nonas, Jonathan Thomas, Mia Westerlund Roosen, and Paul Whiting. I wish to thank Edward Albee and Dr. Harry Rand for their insightful *Context is All: Notes and Conversations*; and special praise is appropriate for Dr. Rand's essay, *What Matters*. I would like to recognize the hard work and dedication to this exhibition project on the part of Anderson Gallery staff: Amy Moorefield, Assistant Director and Curator of Collections; Leon Roper, Gallery and Exhibitions Manager; and student workers Traci Horne and Jessica Colie.

 I would also like to thank the following individuals and organizations that have been important to this project in a number of ways: George Cruger, John Deeds, James Henderson, Jill Weinberg Adams and Lennon, Weinberg, Inc, New York City, NY, Waqas Wajahat and Knoedler and Company, New York, NY, and the New Gallery, Houston. Thanks to Laura Carpenter of Clearwater Productions for producing the video documentation and interviews with Edward Albee and the nine artists. Laura Chessin deserves a special thanks for her wonderful design of this publication. Her enthusiasm for this project and professionalism carried through into her work. We were extremely fortunate to work with Elizabeth Bolka and the staff of Worth Higgins. Their high standards in printing are matched by their patience and excellent advice. A special thanks to Pat Soden, Director, and the dedicated staff of the University of Washington Press for distribution of this publication.

The exhibition and publication have been made possible, in part, through the generous support of VCU's School of the Arts, the Qatar Foundation for Education, Science and Community Development, Doha, Qatar.

Lastly, I wish to thank Dr. Richard Toscan, Dean, School of the Arts, for his encouragement and support.

Really fine sculpture takes us beyond the 'facts' of the material

— metal, wood, whatever —

into metaphor.

Introduction

From Idea to Matter: *Some Thoughts on Sculpture*

The illusion versus the real: this represents the fundamental difference between painting and sculpture. In painting, all is illusion: object, color, shape, perspective. Nothing is "real" beyond the illusion of reality created by the painter. It is, after all, all flat, all false, and, in the best hands, all wonderful, all real. In sculpture, everything is real: object color, shape, perspective, and, in the best hands, all is wonderful and filled with illusion.

It comes down to the reality of illusion versus the illusion of reality.

Really fine sculpture takes us beyond the "facts" of the material— metal, wood, whatever— into metaphor. It takes us beyond the concrete (no pun intended) into the implied, in the same way painting (and drawing, of course) takes us beyond the surface falsity to the suggested reality.

The two work identical if contradictory magics.

Sculpture is less popular than painting, I suspect, because it asks a more complex suspension of disbelief on the part of the viewer or —perhaps— a more adventuresome mind. But sculpture's rewards are in many ways deeper, by way of its vital "presence."

The sculptors in this exhibit come from all over. Four of them are over fifty years old while others are variously younger. While none of them could be said to be household names yet— outside the art world, of course; within they are either very well known or getting there— some of them have established powerful international reputations, while others are certain to do so. And the older four have the freshness of youth, and the younger have a maturity beyond their years.

All of them have certain things in common— besides excellence, sureness, individuality, adventuresomeness— and paramount among them is, certainly, the "hands-on" quality of the work, the clear evidence of the artist making the art— molding, carving, manipulating, intruding. There is no theoretical work here, no work that is merely "idea." It is all worked on, worked through idea to matter.

That all the work is abstract to one degree or another merely states that it is, every piece of it, concerned with something beyond mere representation, and has to do with a redefinition of the nature of representation itself.

Oh, and furthermore, the work is tough and demanding and thrilling and absolutely beautiful.

Edward Albee

New York

August 2000

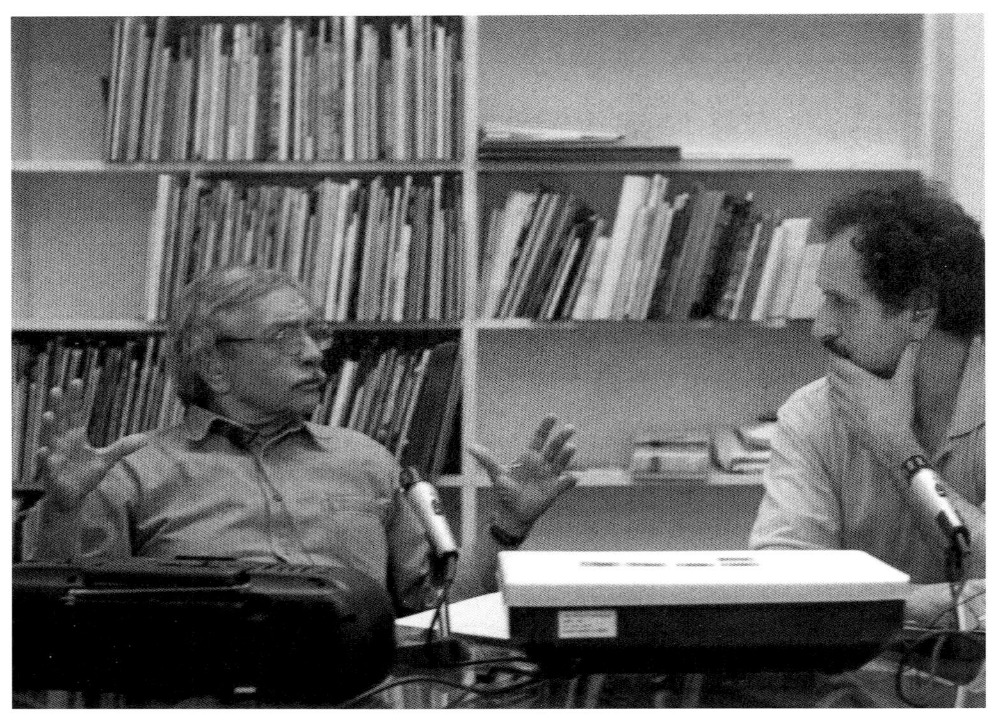

Edward Albee and Harry Rand at Anderson Gallery, Virginia Commonwealth University.

Context is All

Notes and Conversations with Edward Albee and Harry Rand

In July of 2000 Edward Albee and Harry Rand sat down at Anderson Gallery to record the following

"Conversation," concerning Albee's curatorial selections of the nine sculptors included in From *Idea to Matter*.

Albee and Rand had not met before, and no questions were submitted prior to the interview....TP

HR: I want to get some of the show's assumptions made explicit. Did Ted Potter (*Director of Anderson Gallery*) put any constraints on you on who you would choose, or how to choose them?

EA: No, of course not. He knows my taste. He knows the work of some of the artists in the show. He knows the kind of work that I like. I don't know whether he's seen catalogues of previous exhibits that I've curated or not. He may have over the years.

No, no constraints. I imagine if I wanted to exhibit a piece which blew up the museum, he might have had a couple of reservations, though I understand that he wants a new one, so perhaps not.

HR: When you selected these artists, did you choose them with the idea that they might hang well together?

EA: Well, certainly not that they would be contradictory, nor was I after the trendy, which I'm opposed to greatly. The work is abstract, all abstract, all is hands-on work: very specifically, the artists' hands are very visible in all of the work. It strikes me—it's all art about art, about the definition of art.

HR: Yes, which is not at all the same as "art for art's sake". This is art aiming to advance the scope of human understanding, to mention things heretofore not remarked upon, to record or make an incident formerly beneath notice.

In looking over the art, what struck me was that, for an artist who works as you do, there might be a craving for the autographic art: the record of a touch and the art of the touch, as opposed to the precarious position of your work, which you send out into the world, and the plastic imagery is left to directors and actors.[1]

But being a playwright, you're not only a literary artist, but you're a visual artist,

and you're a composer.

It's an auditory experience and a visual experience, as well as a literary experience.

EA: Well, I've never believed that, you see. I don't believe that is the way theater should be going. As a playwright, I started off wanting to be a composer and a visual artist when I was very young. I started doing paintings and drawings when I was quite young. And I discovered Mozart and Bach when I was 11, so I decided I wanted to be a composer. But I failed in those two very, very quickly and very completely.

But being a playwright, you're not only a literary artist, but you're a visual artist, and you're a composer. It's an auditory experience and a visual experience, as well as a literary experience. So, as a playwright, I'm very involved in all three of those things, and I've learned probably as much as any layman knows about classical music over the years, and I know the literature very, very well. And with the visual arts, I started being very interested in the visual arts when I was going to school; I was renting reproductions of Kandinsky and Malevich and those people for my walls when I was 14 and 15 years old. So I've been very interested in the visual arts and became fairly knowledgeable in those. And I think that's helpful to a playwright, but also that's just my nature. I like those three things: literature, and painting and sculpture, and music a lot. They all relate to me very much.

HR: If you see yourself as creating a continuum with the words and music and plastic imagery implicit on the page….

EA: No, what I said was, that I think for a playwright not to have the sensibility for musical composition and the visual arts is a limitation for him. I do think, when I'm writing a play, sometimes I'm writing a string quartet. I'm aware of the sound and the aesthetic similarities. But the visual thing is a little more remote; we do have a set, we do have an environment, and I'm very specific about the background I'd like for the plays. We have objects, sculptural objects, standing in position and moving, rather in the way that we would dance at the same time. It helps, I think, if you're going to be talking to lighting designers and set designers, it helps to have some awareness. I'm more interested always in dance setting than in the usual dramatic setting, unless you have the naturalistic play like *Virginia Woolf* where I want a cluttered living room.

HR: Do you think it works the other way? Do you think these artists have implicit in their work rhythms and cadences that are like speech and like drama?

EA: No, I wouldn't go that far. I've never thought of it in those terms. No, I'm not trying to relate any of this work to my work. That's not the intention of this show.

HR: I didn't know if it was, but I wanted to know if…

EA: Oh, goodness, no. No, no. I would imagine that my affection for the work helped determine my choices. I wouldn't like it so much unless I'd felt an aesthetic, not similarity, but congeniality. I don't know that one would go to see this show and say, "That's Edward Albee's mind there." Maybe, to a certain extent, but more his taste.

HR: I was thinking of the "wrong end of the telescope" sensation, where you can start with words and unpack from that rhythms and cadences and music, and therefore dance arises and therefore plastic imagery….

EA: I think you'd be stretching it too far. I think you'd be constructing a case that might have validity, but it's beside the point here.

HR: That may account for your success as a playwright, whereas a visual artist might see the world in the visual, including all of those other—not necessarily synesthetic, but compacted and analogous—sensations.

EA: Yeah. But I don't want you to be coming to the conclusion that I like this work only because it relates to the way I work or I think.

HR: Not at all.

EA: The work is so dissimilar. It's the way I feel about sculpture. Now, obviously I'm not going to have any work that I'm not sympathetic to, right? Of course not.

HR: And there are deep sympathies.

EA: Yeah. There's a lot of stuff you can admire and not be sympathetic to, and a lot of stuff you can be sympathetic to that you don't much admire. It's nice to be able to put the two of them together.

HR: Right, that's an adult sensibility and also a professional sensibility. The public doesn't generally understand the difference between the good and what you like.

EA: No, of course not, no. Well, the trick is that you should like what's good.

HR: There's certainly a historical pedigree for this kind of work. No one starts off from scratch with this. It's intelligent work.

EA: Oh, everybody comes from somebody. You have to come from somebody.

HR: Picasso had a great line about that, that you probably know. He said something like: "In life, it's not considered an honor not to have a father. Why should it be in art?"

EA: Exactly, yes.

HR: There's a lot of history and memory in these pieces.

EA: And that's something very interesting about Picasso, by the way, and I think someday people are going to realize how much more important his sculpture is than a lot of people do now. Because I think he didn't really do a painting that mattered much after about 1932, and a lot of the sculpture after that is wonderful.

HR: Yeah. Starting in the 1920s, when he rethinks abstraction, he becomes a different artist, and I think the two bodies of his work are underrated.[2]

EA: It actually began in that period of 1931 and 1932 when he was doing the figures on the beach which he ended up doing as sculptures. That's a very interesting transition.

HR: That starts 1927-29. I think the sculptures and the lino cuts are two underrated bodies of work.[3] Everyone thinks the linocuts are unimportant because kids do linoleum cut prints at camp, so how important can they be. But the linocuts of the 1950s really unite his visual virtuosity with the clarity of graphic device.

EA: I love his sculpture a lot.

HR: Are the artists in the show artists you personally collect?

EA: Yeah, but then again, that's hardly a limitation, since I have a lot of stuff. Do I have work by all these people? Yeah, sure. I have two pieces of **John Duff**'s that are from 1972, early fiberglass wall pieces. I've known a some of these artists, **John Duff** and **Mia Westerlund Roosen** and **Richard Nonas**, for a very long time. And **Jonathan Thomas** a long time, too. But some of them are like **John Beech**, whose work I became aware of in San Francisco about 10 years ago, when he was a very young artist out there. **David Fulton** is a Houston artist. **Barry Goldberg** is working very quietly in Brooklyn; no one pays any attention to him, which is too bad. **David McDonald** is a West Coast artist also, whose work I saw out there. And **Paul Whiting** was a core fellow down at the University of Houston four years ago.[4]

HR: Are you an inveterate gallery-goer?

EA: Yes, I go to galleries constantly, all the time.

HR: And did you see these pieces in your gallery explorations or do they represent recommendations from friends?

EA: I go to studios, too. It's very interesting, in that I see things hang in a way that most people don't usually see them. I remember back in 1940-something, I went to the then Museum of Nonobjective Art.

HR: What is now the Guggenheim Museum in New York.[5]

EA: Before it was the Guggenheim. It was on 52nd or 53rd Street, between Park and Madison on the second floor, run by Hilla Rebay at that time.[6] And the sculptor who did *The Endless House*, Frederick Keisler, had hung a show there, and almost everything was just a foot above the floor. It was very interesting to see.

HR: It's a way to break through the visitor's complacency. You start thinking about space, which is what sculpture is all about: to make you think about space.

EA: And I think things should be hung up near the ceiling and on the floor and odd places.

The work is so dissimilar.

It's the way *I feel* about sculpture.

Now, obviously I'm not going to have any work that I'm not sympathetic to, right?

Of course not.

HR: As long as you can make the sculpture be sensible.

EA: Yeah, that's right. But the stuff having to be at a level where people have to see it either sitting down or standing is very strange to me.

HR: It's literally a kind of pedestrian view of things.

EA: I mean, stuff that's meant to be on the floor, you can only put it on the floor. Or if it's small enough, on a table. But if it's very small and wants to be on the floor and doesn't want to be on the table, you put it on the floor.

HR: And there have been problems about that. When Anthony Caro was trying to figure out how to do the table pieces, the only thing he could think of to make them ultimately only table pieces was to have something, some element of the work, hanging off, and then it could only be a table piece.[7] And of course the Richard Serra pieces you can leave on the floor, and the Andre pieces, using weight and gravity in different ways.[8]

I have a personal theory that sculptors mature a lot later than painters. It takes a lot longer to make each individual sculpture, so it takes longer to make your first 5,000 mistakes, but in general if—and this is my premise—painters come into their own and really mature at 40, sculptors generally do it around 60. Not that I intend that this man should suffer ignominiously until he's 60, but they hit their stride later on.

EA: Well, some painters, too, of course. Mark Rothko never saw the painting until he was in his fifties.[9]

HR: Barnett Newman really didn't have his first show until he was almost 40, but that was a different time.[10]

EA: Well, here's one — you can ask him about his work.

HR: Jonathan Thomas? [who has just entered the room]

EA: Yeah.

HR: No, I want to ask the curator.

EA: What are you putting in the show, the totems? About 35 of the totems?

HR: Would you ever know that a mathematician made these?

EA: Yeah, Jonathan Thomas studied pure mathematics in Canada.

HR: I'd like to ask each of you the same question, since we do have the luxury of having the artist and the curator in the same room, and that is: Do you have a preference for seeing these in larger or smaller masses of groupings?

EA: They're totally different in their effect.

JT: No, as far as I'm concerned, the piece is 30 pieces.

EA: I think he's relating it to what Louise Nevelson said to me about her stuff once: Louise said: "Every piece I've ever done is part of a big piece." And then when she did Mrs. N.'s Palace we saw exactly what she meant by that. Everything was knitting, also. Stitching, she meant everything was stitching.

JT: When people put together groups of 3 or 5, it's fine, but, you know, I'd love 30, since I think that's complete.

EA: I was helping to put together a show that Jonathan had in Chicago at Roy Boyd's Gallery a couple of years ago, and he had several groups of 15, 17, but there was one little niche that was very interesting: I took 3 of the smaller ones, 1 white one and 2 black ones, and put them on a stand this high from the floor, of the taller white one and the two black ones in a little niche all by themselves, and it's a totally different effect. They work in small groups.

JT: I like other people interacting with work and putting groups together. I like that.

HR: When you see the large aggregates, you get two sensations; at least, I get two sensations. One of them is that there's a sculptural statement being made, a commitment to a specific rhythmic cadence, but the other one is that there's that sensation of seeing a cultural statement that only time and aggregation can produce. Like when you go to see these Dogon sites in Africa or indeed any culture, where you get this affirmation time and time again, and you get that commitment. And it's something that's lacking from a lot of modern art, where the single statement is supposed to carry all that weight, all that cultural weight, rather than committing to repetition and really make a very definite commitment. I realize that I'm using that word twice, but…

EA: John relates a lot of his work to the non-anthropomorphic, to geometry and pure mathematics.

JT: Well, when I started out, I thought I was doing a visual representation of the hypertext, because I kind of wanted it to go over and lead every thing; every sequence of events would lead to another sequence. And you could bounce around and your eye would go across and follow the different themes, but it ended up not being about that. It's really about the two extremes, and how things repeat across….

HR: But all good art is hypertext. You know, Basil Bunting asserted that poetry comes from dance and you keep a certain cadence in music, in musical background at least, in the writing.[11] Not necessarily in the voices of the personae in the plays, but in your own sense of composition.

EA: Sure. It's the fact that you can conduct a play when you're directing it.

HR: Right. There's an orchestral shape, there's a form, and you have a sense of completeness when you leave the theater. There's got to have been a form, however unknown to the audience, however separate from the obvious dramatic intentions.

EA: Have you ever been to Mexico City?

HR: Never.

EA: Under Mexico City, under the center of Mexico City, under the main square near the cathedral, they've excavated an Aztec city, and there is a wall of skulls that they've found. It's about 12 feet by 10 feet, and it is a wall of skulls.[12]

HR: A representation of a skull rack.

JT: And he thinks I may have gotten the idea for presenting the ovals from that, but I didn't.

EA: But the New Guinea work, when you see that…

HR: Yeah, Sepic River work from New Guinea. You get that sense of them.

EA: You do, yeah.

HR: And there's a great value to having that repetition.

EA: And that was a moving experience for you [directed to Jonathan Thomas], seeing that wall.

JT: Oh, it was. It was beautiful.

EA: Whether it related specifically to this stuff or not is hard to say.

HR: And one never does know where it comes out.

EA: Exactly. You're not often sure where you're getting the stuff from. Jonathan wants to have the totems in the show rather than the newer work that he's doing.

JT: You know you were talking earlier of the futurists and all that. That's a big feel of his collection. So, you do have a big interest in Moholy-Nagy and all that.

EA: In the construction, yeah, I like that. But then again, I have a lot of African stuff, too.

HR: Which is the wellspring of so much modern sculpture. Maybe all modern sculpture.

HR: Have you ever done visual art yourself?

EA: Not since I was 12 or 13.

HR: Did you ever get ideas for pieces looking at other people's?

EA: No. No, I knew I would be imitative and not very good. I mean, I can turn out a perfectly good constructivist wall piece – fake, but o.k.

HR: There's something to be said for a highly refined sensibility in any art. It gets carried over. Michelangelo wrote important poetry.

EA: No. It's essential. One of the reasons that I'm happy that I have my Foundation is that it provides working and living space for writers and painters and sculptors; these people get so insulated: sculptors talk to sculptors, writers talk to writers, they're thrown out there in my Foundation all mixed together, and they get to relate to each other, and they learn more about each other's aesthetic. And maybe they start relating more, which is the point.

HR: There are things in each of the arts that can be analogized to the others. There's a core sensibility in each art.

EA: Well, obviously you know a great deal about the theater yourself. What conclusions do you come to from what you look at here?

HR: Well, I see myself in an interesting situation. Normally, I'm curator of the show. It's my sensibility that weeds out from the larger possibilities a subset of everything that's possible within the limits of what is presented or available, and the subset, first of all, will always be my sensibility, and sometimes have even a philosophical underpinning. Because as you know, there are a couple of things you can do: you can hang a room so that it looks well together—decoration. You can show some sort of chronological progress—history, which is not always a logical. Or if you want to you can even have some idea; the idea can be about order, or art or about politics—logic or rational relationships. In this case, I found myself in a really interesting situation. Talking to the curator, and I can only imagine that my job is to bring an art historical veneer to a sensibility….

EA: A rough-hewn sensibility, I trust.

HR: No, not yours. Your sensibility is highly polished. And I'm going to have to pretend that in you there's the professional art historical background and method and mechanism that's lacking, which probably isn't the case. Because most of the time, amateurs, true amateurs, know more than the professionals, since the professionals are obligated to abject themselves to the crap of the profession. *(continued next page)*

HR *(continued)*: My brother, who as you know is a painter, knows a great deal more about parts of art history than I do, because he's not obligated to read the whole bibliography. He can just read the good stuff. Filleted art history. I can't afford to fillet art history, to not know the internal mechanisms of bibliography and method.

EA: When people do photographs of my loft and of the art in it and stuff like that, they refer to a collection. And I say, no, I'm not a collector, I'm an accumulator. I accumulate stuff that I relate to.

HR: There's a big difference, because a collection has a point.

EA: Yes, and most of these days, are put together by other people, not by the owners.

HR: I've met very few collectors of the recent generation because most of them are really investors who call themselves collectors.

EA: That's right.

HR: You're really a collector, which means you don't have a collection, you have an accumulation.

EA: Yeah, exactly, yes.

HR: And it's the truest expression of affection.

EA: And I'll even have areas where I have a wonderful piece of sculpture up and somebody will say, "Gee, that's really a beautiful piece. Who did that?" And I have to admit that it was part of a railway tie that somebody has put on a stand. It becomes art when that happens to it.

HR: Sure, it is transparent.

EA: And that can stand perfectly well next to anything.

HR: Which says a lot about our time.

EA: Well, I think it says a lot about how things become art. I mean, after all, the African stuff isn't made as art.

HR: Right, which says a lot about our moment in history. Our era is the inheritor of Japanese contextualism and the rough-hewn sensibility of Africa as opposed to the polish of beaux-art with which African collided in the early part of the 20th century—within the fashionable context of Japonisme.[13]

EA: There is something that makes something art, and it doesn't have anything to do with historicism. It doesn't have anything to do with anything except the piece itself is art in context. I remember I saw an exhibit about 25 years ago. Beautifully lighted, beautifully hung. They were basically geometric, all slightly different; some of them sort of rough on the edges. And I looked at them for a few minutes and I realized what they were. They were a very, very shrewd collection of manhole covers that had been transformed into art by saying, "take them out of that context and put them into another context."

You know there's a wonderful thing they have on New York streets that look like Richard Serra's, great huge rectangular steel plates with a hook thing on the end and maybe a couple of symbols in them? They are such beautiful pieces of sculpture.

HR: But Serra taught us to see that.

EA: No, I'm not sure if it doesn't work both ways. I don't think that we saw them as sculpture only after Serra. I think that maybe we saw them as sculpture because of all art, not just because Serra did similar stuff.

HR: But you have to have a prepared sensibility. You know, people make the mistake—or at least, it's the popular [mis]conception—that artistic geniuses have feelings that other people don't have. That geniuses feel differently, feel more and unconventional emotions. It's not true. Nobody would go to a Beethoven performance if they didn't understand the feelings. The genius is having the obsession, being so out of your mind with a compulsion to do it. Whether it's your compulsion, or my compulsion or somebody else's, to do it. Most people let a brief emotion without a name pass by. Whereas the popular sensibility may have been sufficiently alerted to the happenstance of those steel plates, you needed a Serra to put it in front of you, to validate it. And I would think that process is what comes out of a…

EA: So am I saying to myself, did I think those were art pieces before I saw my first Serra or not? I don't know. It's just as likely that I saw them as art pieces before I saw Serra.

HR: There are fleeting sensibilities that get captured by being contextualized as art, and then we can have a handle on it. That process of thinking has nothing to do with quality, per se, but has to do with the self-consciousness of context, which probably comes out of the occidental experience of Japan in the late 19th and early 20th centuries. And even today there are things that you can talk about as art in Japan that you can't do in the West, because for us art has to be an artifact, a thing made. The Japanese have "moon viewing parties" where the reaction that you're having is the art. It's not the moon; the moon stays up there and is not made by anybody. And when we finally come to that, that the self-consciousness of our aesthetic experience…

EA: …and context is all.

HR: Yeah. Yes, that could summarize our discussion.

EA: That's the title to your piece: "Context is All". Or mine.

HR: Or yours.

JT: A lot of the things that you have been interested in, you go beyond what is just the object itself, because you're dealing with personalities because you know many people. I mean, would you really collect Milton Avery today?

EA: I saw Milton's work first—before he became terribly famous—- and went to his studio….

JT: But maybe you were just educating yourself.

EA: Maybe I was. I ended up with 5 or 6 of Milton's paintings. I paid 500 or 600 bucks for work out of his studio a long time ago. I like them. I'm not embarrassed at having some Milton Averys, I think they're very beautiful things.

HR: Oddly enough, the very first Milton Avery painting ever sold was to a performing artist. A man named Louis Kaufman, who was a violinist.

JT: I mean, don't you think that, because you're a creative person, and you know a lot of creative persons, that some of what you're interested in comes out of just that process.

EA: It may. I remember I used to like Matisse a lot, and Milton came out of Matisse. Colorists came out of Matisse, and Mark Rothko's color sense came out of Milton Avery, because Mark admired Milton enormously.

HR: As a matter of fact, Rothko was introduced to Avery by this fellow Louis Kaufman. They had never met before.

EA: Really? How interesting.

HR: Kaufman was an interesting fellow. A musician of the highest caliber. During the Depression, he moved to Los Angeles, and he did studio work—the music tracks for movies—because it was steady work. He plays the violin solos in *Gone With the Wind* and dozens of other movies. With the result that, because he got a paycheck every week, he could perform experimental work on the side and had a string quartet. And everyone—Stravinsky and Milhaud—everyone wrote for him. He made the first recording of Vivaldi's The Four Seasons, and innumerable 20th century pieces, some written for him.

EA: Yes, of course.

HR: He told me he had bought the very first Avery for $25, and that he also had known Rothko, because like you he haunted artists' studios, and said to Rothko this Avery fellow was someone you really ought to meet.[14] His wife and long-time piano accompanist, Annette, still lives in Los Angeles, with the few pictures she and Louis haven't given to museums.

EA: There's a book out that you might want to look at that has the loft in it. What's the book called? *Living with Art*.

JT: We do tease Edward for buying bad examples of people's work, because he does like those odd pieces.

EA: Well, as an example, the only Chagall that I have is a 1908 portrait of his sister reading a book, and it relates to the one in Basel which was painted about 3 years later. It doesn't have the flying people or even those colors that Chagall got into eventually. It's an early piece and it's a very beautiful painting. And I say: Guess who that is? And nobody knows it's a Chagall. And they say you're kidding. Where are all the kissing people and flying shit? Because I thought he was a very wonderful

artist between about 1907 and 1915, a marvelous, serious tough artist. But then he got commercial with it.

HR: That's an interesting case, what happens to people as they soften, because it also happened to Kees Van Dongen and to Raoul Dufy. People forget that, at the turn of the century, Dufy was shoulder-to-shoulder with Braque. At the cutting edge. But artists come to the precipice, and they look down and some of them get scared.

EA: One of the oddest histories of famous work is Picabia.[15] I saw a Picabia from about 1918, not very ornate, but in a gold frame, and all it was—you could see right through it to the back wall—there were some vertical, horizontal and diagonal strings, some of which had been tied together with little cardboard squares, but it was a beautiful, an extraordinary painting, as wonderful as anything that [Marcel] Duchamp did or Joseph Beuys did—two artists that I think are particularly important and that I admire a lot.

HR: And in some ways more difficult, because the precedent for doing less hadn't been there. When, some years ago, the Barnes collection hit the road and came to Washington, for the first time you could see the *Bonheur de Vie*, because when it's at home at the Barnes Foundation in Merion, Pennsylvania, it's at the top of a stairwell.[16] If you take a step forward to look at it, you break your neck. It's part of their perversity. And so when it travelled, for the first time I was able to walk up and examine it. And I saw how various and how rough some of the brushwork is. The heroism of that piece is not the composition or its vibrant color or its scale, but that Matisse could step back from it and say, "Ok, that's done," at a time when there was no precedent at all—not even a position from which you could analogize—that this would be a finished painting. I spent a lot of time looking at it trying to figure out how he could have decided this was done.

Well, not only affection, I think, but . . .
Useful affection.

EA: Another wonderful artist that nobody pays too much attention to anymore, but of course so much of his work got destroyed
in São Päulo, is Torres-García.[17] You know, his sculpture especially.
It's good stuff.

HR: Torres-García is important because he was the one who
taught us how to read and look at the same time. Or to alternate
or oscillate between reading and looking on the same surface.

EA: But his 3-dimensional work, even more than his paintings,
his sculpture to me is amazing.

HR: The early Adolph Gottliebs, the "pictographs", come out
of that.[18]

EA: Well, his transitional stuff, yeah, is surrealist in the Torres-
García manner before he moved into the final stuff. Much better,
tougher work. Watching all of those painters work—watching
Pollock, watching Mark Rothko—all of them moving through their
surrealist thing…. It's fascinating.

HR: It was an apprenticeship of attractive emotions.

EA: There was a very interesting exhibit in Houston, Texas, at the
Menil in their surrealist collection—a huge surrealist collection—-
a room there, and I forget what they called the exhibition. It was
of things that were accumulated by the surrealist artists, sort of
similar to the early African work collected by the cubists. But it
was just stuff that surrealists were collecting, an extraordinary
assemblage of unlikely things.

HR: Things constellated by affection. Things of affection.

EA: Well, not only affection, I think, but useful. Useful affection.

HR: Artistically useful?

EA: Oh, yeah. Of course.

HR: And is that what your collection is?

EA: I have no idea. My accumulation?

HR: Is it aesthetically accumulated for artistic use?

EA: I can't think in those terms. I find it very difficult to think
about myself or my work from the third person. I can't look at
it and say what affect does it have or what does it need. I can't
do that.

HR: Do you examine the sources of your work?

EA: I know what they are, sure. Some of them that I admire a lot,
some that I have a great love for and admire so much. I know
where I come from, sure, but I come from so many different
sources. I mean, we can start back with the Greeks and work right
up to the present. O'Neil's work—when I was a teenager, I saw
A Long Day's Journey and *The Iceman Cometh* for the first time
when I was 16, and it knocked me out. A lot of stuff did. Seeing
Tennessee Williams, all those people when I was a teenager, being
exposed to the French avant-garde which I was reading before I
started seeing the plays, reading Sartre and Camus and all of those
people back when I was 15 or 16 years old. All that stuff ties in.
And, of course, Beckett. But, then again, I don't know what any of
it means.

HR: Well, there's also the question: do one's sources ever close off,
or as you begin to accumulate experiences….

EA: They shouldn't.

HR: Yes, they shouldn't, but people, as you know, run out of steam.

EA: I see the artists' sources closing off far too often. I think later in the career, even somebody who did as much good work as Diebenkorn did, finally. I said: ok, he's hit it, he's hit the good stuff, and he's just going to go on with it. But that happens to a lot of them.

HR: That was attenuated. But you don't know if that's fear or if it's sensible, because unless you really make something your own, unless you kill it so no one else can take it over, it's not yours.

EA: But it's not your own anymore if you're doing it just for commerce.

JT: But some people create their own world and keep enlarging it.

EA: Yeah, but that's insularity, through retreat from the field, because you're not allowing yourself to be open to influence anymore.

HR: And so, while we hope that you're open to influence, the question is really: does the accumulation of affectionate objects, do you think it works on you in some way? Both as a human being and an artist.

EA: Certainly I like to be surrounded by stuff I like to look at. I'm sure it's probably still having some sort of effect, or if it doesn't have any effect anymore, put it in the closet and put something else up.

HR: It's self-curating.

EA: Sure.

HR: We've talked about selecting the objects for this show and your sensibility and historical background behind those choices, and the selection of found objects, but we haven't talked about installation. Because as a curator, what you're going to be doing is mounting these works, and there are different ways to mount things. You can mount them to, as we say, to make a room look harmonious, i.e., decorating. You can make a point historically. You could mount them to illustrate some idea.

EA: This is more—don't put too much in the room—that each piece exhibit itself. You can have a piece that fills the whole wall, and that's fine. Or you can have a small piece this size that needs an entire wall. You have to know how much space each piece needs, and if you're putting two people in the same room, how different do you make them. I don't know how that works as relating or vibrating aesthetic experiences. But I don't like to put too much in a room. I don't know, I'd try to isolate each of these artists from the other.

HR: That aesthetic seems so obvious to us today, because it's also a contemporary taste. It's certainly not the cluttered aesthetic of the Victorian "Brown Decades" or the Rococo. For example, two weeks ago, I found myself in Versailles, for the first time since I was a kid. I took my daughter there. And when I saw it as a boy, I thought it was oppressive, fascistic and leaden, so I never bothered to go back. And I took this 10 year old little girl, and it looked exactly the same way. It's such a fist in your face, and it was meant to be different from our sense of priority or individuality.

or if it doesn't have any effect anymore, put it in the closet and put something else up.

EA: The English townhouses, the English country houses, too.

HR: Just heaps of stuff. All that labor invested just heaped up and thrown at you as a show of wealth. And it was the aesthetic of being well-off as opposed to those who weren't. It's so different from the aesthetic that you talk about and that we take more or less for granted: let the art speak as an individual object, rather than being subsumed into some ensemble.

EA: I wish we had 9 rooms here at the Anderson Gallery so I could have one artist in each room. We don't quite have 9 rooms, so a couple of them I'm going to have to put together. Put as much space around them as they need.

HR: The idea of space that a work "needs" arises or seems reasonable to us because we see artists as individuals, not part of a choir speaking for society. It's obvious to you, it's obvious to me, but it's something of the moment. Of an extended moment.

EA: So I don't know that there's any governing thing in this accumulation of art. It's just some artists that I think are good and interesting and more people should be paying attention to.

HR: Ok. It's salutary.

EA: I don't have to know an artist to like them, to know an artist to accumulate them.

HR: And you also have a personal relationship with some of them, you participate in their creative lives, critically.

EA: Mia Westerlund Roosen was doing big concrete pieces on the floor, and I said to her one day: why don't you lean one of them over against the wall? And that changed everything for her. But now, of course, she says: It was inevitable that her work would rise from the floor and be leaning against the wall.

HR: Inevitable as long as you are the instrument of the zeitgeist. And that brings us back to, "would we have known that these steel plates were art if there wasn't a Carl Andre," and chances are we would have had an aesthetic intuition, but it wouldn't have been in the intent of art.

EA: Probably not. But I don't remember having lots of debates with artists. [to Thomas] I try to tell you what to do all the time.

JT: He's notorious for going into studios and saying, "It's done. Leave it."

EA: That's because so many artists keep working on a piece and fuck it up completely.

HR: Part of it's economics, unfortunately. If you don't sell a work, it's there to bash around. It's strange: people talk about young artists being "heroic" or "revolutionary," but it's much easier to be an effective revolutionary when you're already a successful artist because you know people will stop and look and pay attention. They will consider your work and give you the benefit of the doubt because they know you are earnest and worth the extra attention. And you can take a bit of risk; the audience will take it seriously. They will go further with you before doubting.

EA: I go to studios and somebody has something that is clearly a finished piece, and it's so busy, so static, because it's finalized. And I see something they're working on, and I just know that if they don't do one more thing it's going to be a more exciting piece. I try to tell them not to do it, not to go any further. Take chances.

HR: Do you tell them to stop painting? "Stop painting that picture." It's the enthusiastic observer.

EA: Well, I'm a busybody. I like to show people what to do. They don't pay any attention to me, anyway.

HR: That's probably because you're articulate. Other people might have intuitions about what they like and not like and not know why. More here, more there. People don't know why they like things and don't like them. Nobody really knows ultimately why they like and don't like things; they can't express their dissatisfactions. They haven't thought about them.

JT: The saddest thing is when people stop working because they physically can't go on, Lee Krasner and people like that who just couldn't do it anymore. They just stopped.

EA: Yeah, because of arthritis. Very sad.

HR: Adolph Gottlieb had a stroke in 1964, and afterwards he was able to delegate some of the work to assistants. You can see a difference in the pictures, but because so much of his art had to do with placement and coloring, the mixing of hues and paint, he could give adequate instructions, even from a wheelchair. The pictures could continue. And that's very different from, say, having other people paint your pictures for you. It's a heck of a difference.

EA: Yeah.

. . . there's a great virtue to the hand,

HR: And it comes down to what you can offload onto someone else. Lord knows architecture is the best example of that.

EA: Interesting what happened to Henry Moore. He would make this little maquette, and then he would have his assistants make one twice the size and then 4 times and end up 16 times the size. The things would normally go from 2 to 4 to 8 to 16. The works looked different as a result.

HR: And when you don't make adjustments for scale—and you can tell this clearly in sculpture—very often pieces suffer dramatically. I did some work some years ago on Paul Manship, and I started studying different versions he made of pieces, sometimes in 4 sizes.[19] He was a good enough sculptor to make adjustments in each size. He wasn't simply turning his work over to the assistant or foundry and saying enlarge this 5 times the size. He'd go back and change things, because you know the spectator's point of view is going to be different, because the mass is going to feel different in relation to the viewer's body. I think it's going to take a long time for that kind of craftsmanship to be noticed and to come back in fashion when we're doing so much art which is rightfully minimalist, rightfully conceptual, rightfully contextual, as opposed to displaying virtuosity and craftsmanship. The two can co-exist, but rarely at the same time, the same place. Only in our heads, the museum without walls.

to the artist's visibility.

EA: Yeah, but there's a great virtue to the hand, to the artist's visibility.

HR: It's astonishing what will not lend itself to computer manipulation. I was talking to Clement Meadmore a few years ago, and you'd think that of any artist, his pieces, particularly the large metal prismatic things, you could just set up a computer to do all the variations and then look at the ones that work, like a menu. He says he can't. You've actually got to work with the forms and model them, and see what works, check scale, check angles, and how it's going to be viewed. That makes him a superior artist, ethically, but the pay-off is that his works are remarkably successful.

EA: Did you notice that with the maquettes?

HR: I think the maquettes are conceived with the idea of seeing them at a certain size. You can't generate them on a computer and just turn them around. I thought you could save yourself a lot of work if you could compose a piece and then just tell the computer do every variation, and set up some sort of algorithm.

EA: I saw something much more interesting, wonderful, about 5 or 6 years ago in London. It was an exhibit of Franz Kline's big black and white paintings. Right next to each one of them—which I hadn't known he'd done—was a preliminary drawing.

HR: There wasn't a square inch of improvisation in his pictures.

EA: Startlingly.

HR: He's a great academic or traditional artist, and his paint handling is accurate. People don't understand that about him.

EA: It was startling. I thought that when he worked on everything, he did them that way.

HR: You know who's got a wonderful collection of those Kline drawings is Cy Twombly.

EA: Cy has a collection of them? Now there's a person whose sculpture I admire more than half of his paintings, Cy. I love his sculpture. They're beautiful things. But that was fascinating to me, Kline, because I thought those were gestural paintings.

HR: He's as spontaneous as Degas. Every inch is planned and laid out. And there are versions of different pictures, and you can see him working on them. When you see the finished pictures, you can often see that he's working against gravity. The canvases have been rotated 2 or 3 times, which you can tell from the way the paint has dripped.

EA: That doesn't change the experience, because the piece exists on its own terms. But maybe it was a little more exciting when I thought it was all chance, when a lot of chances were being taken with the big brush and the big stuff.

HR: But that raises an interesting question about where the excitement of any kind of work comes from. As you know, Glen Gould gave up performing because he called it "a blood sport." People were sitting around waiting for a wrong note. Why should you have to be on the spot on any given night when you've got the ability to record it? Does that change the nature of the performing art? Well, of course, it does.

EA: The difference between the sound of a live performance and the sound of a recording, of course.

HR: Or the difference between play and film.

EA: Well, no, that's a different difference.

HR: A recording of a performance of a piece of music can be done in a number of takes and edited together….

EA: I know it can.

HR: You're irritated by that?

EA: A little bit, yeah.

HR: Seems inauthentic?

EA: Yeah. I know they do it, of course.

HR: Does that mean that you find improvisation exciting? The risk, the spontaneity, the revelation, confessionally then?

EA: Yes.

HR: Unless it's highly conventional….

EA: It's called rehearsing your ad libs which apparently is what Franz Kline did.

HR: Well, I'm thinking about an art such as Indian classical music, where the melody and rhythms are highly structured so that it is possible to improvise but only within a fairly rigorous system. I'm not sure if you're familiar with this….

EA: Yeah, I know the music. I know where Philip Glass comes from and where he should go back to.

HR: We can erase that comment if you want to.

EA: I don't mind. Keep it in.

HR: Keep it in? It's OK with me. I find such work offensive. I don't understand how anybody gets nourished on that aesthetic.

EA: I don't either.

HR: Particularly when you do, for instance, know Indian music, which is one of the richest artistic traditions in the world, and by virtue of having so rigorously conventionalized what you can and cannot do.

EA: I find Glass pretty offensive.

HR: And that will be interesting, because people looking at the art in this show, who are not conversant with modern art, modernism, may also find the visual minimalism of it insufficiently nourishing.

EA: See, I don't find it particularly minimal, except in the sense that maybe less is more, but it's not minimal in the usual geometric sense.

HR: The art that you've selected I don't find minimal, either. But it may be because it comes informed by a lot of experiences that you bring to it, that I bring to it, that a lot of other people bring to it, and some of that experience is comparative. I know a lot of other examples of it. And some of it is purely the experience of looking, so that you can take smaller and smaller incidents and find them more and more nourishing. But I'm not sure what an uninformed audience will bring to it, and that's what's interesting, because, as you know, there will be some quotient of this audience who will come by virtue of your celebrity. And Lord knows what they're going to make of this. I hope they come out of the show educated and elevated.

EA: I hope so, and I hope some of them will be. My most recent play in Houston has a little nudity in it. And there's one couple – and I'm convinced that it's the same couple who comes back every single night, walks out at the first sight of a breast. One elderly couple—I know it's a different couple each night, but it amuses me to think that it's the same couple who comes back so they can walk out. And there are going to be some people who see this show and say this isn't art. What does it mean?

And I've never understood this comment about art: what does it mean?

The same way that no two people see the same play, because no two people

bring the same experience, the same intelligence,the same open-mindedness,

no two people get the same thing out of a piece of art.

That's what my adopted mother used to say. She'd come to the house and see a good black and white Kandinsky, and she'd say, "What does it mean? I don't know what it means." And I've never understood this comment about art: what does it mean? The same way that no two people see the same play, because no two people bring the same experience, the same intelligence, the same open-mindedness, no two people get the same thing out of a piece of art.

HR: Do you really say that with sincerity that you didn't understand her question or that same question when other people ask it?

EA: No, I don't understand the question, because I don't know what is expected and what is asked.

HR: I always thought that people wanted some sort of obvious moral quotient from their art.

EA: Well, they want something recognizable. The more art moves away from realism to abstraction, they get in trouble, these people.

HR: They don't have the same problem with Bach or Beethoven.

EA: Don't confuse the recognizable with the moral. They don't listen to Bach or Beethoven that much. They prefer Tchaikovsky and Puccini. I mean, Puccini is a fine composer. Tchaikovsky wrote some good music, too. But they're not Bach and Beethoven.

HR: So melody takes up the function of a moral component. That's what Stravinsky said: melody is the most artificial thing in music.

EA: And he had some pretty melodic periods, didn't he?

HR: Yeah the Firebird, you can whistle that going down the street.

EA: Well, take Persephone, take a lot of the ballets. Melody, melody, melody. Of course, he was also using a lot of other people's melodies, too.

HR: And we began this by your confession of your own melodic interest.

EA: Well, I wanted to be a composer. I tell my playwrighting students—I don't teach playwrighting, I have playwrighting workshops at the University of Houston every spring—in theory, at least, you should begin every day listening to a couple of Bach preludes and fugues. It clarifies the mind.

HR: And insinuates a subliminal structure.

EA: Yes, a sense of order. It's always been one of my big arguments about why the National Endowment is hated so much by so many of the know-nothings in Congress, because an aesthetic education allows people to think politically more coherently.

HR: Yeah. Ezra Pound observed that very early on, and if it weren't for his actual politics, he'd be taught in elementary schools in this country. An unfortunate human being and a great artist. It's absolutely true: once your art starts decaying, once you get fuzzy about the art, then rhetoric decays, which means that politicians have a free hand to do whatever they want, because the language no longer means anything. And we've seen that.

EA: Yeah, too much.

HR: The first real deconstructivism came in politics, not in academia.

JT: Why are you so against narrative art, or narrative painting? A lot of people—I mean, a playwright's doing a show, there'll be something about the word.

EA: They're different arts.

JT: No, you really hate narrative painting that has a story.

EA: I don't hate it. I don't relate to it. It doesn't do anything to me for the most part.

JT: People may think that there might be something to do with the spoken word or something in your show that you might curate about art.

EA: Why anybody would *assume* that —since I'm a writer, I'd be interested in art that had words in it? I just find that the ideas in abstraction are so much more fertile and non-limiting than the ideas in representation.

HR: Particularly at this moment. There will be a time when abstraction will probably be as limiting and exhausted a set of possibilities as doing something as social-realist as *The Oath of the Horatii* today.[20] It will feel leaden, and it will feel associated with a moral-political climate that may be repugnant. I don't foresee it, but it does seem to be one of those historical inevitabilities as the pendulum swings.

EA: Yeah, but I think maybe politically. I mean, look at the way the Soviets reacted against their serious art and destroyed it.

HR: What a disaster. In 1921, they closed the door on modern art.

EA: Yeah, that's right, and Shostakovich at home writing his quartets, sitting quietly.

HR: It's a very small recompense for a tremendous burden of human misery.

EA: Of course.

HR: And also other lost art.

EA: And the poets they killed and all the rest of it. And it was the serious artists that got it in the neck. But I don't hate narrative art. There is some that is very good. I just don't want to spend much time with it.

Why anybody would *assume* that—

since I'm a writer, I'd be interested in art that had words in it?

Notes

1. The designation of an autographic art comes from the discussions of Nelson Goodman (specifically his important book *Languages of Art*), who writes that,"a work of art is autographic if and only if the distinction between original and forgery of it is significant… thus painting is autographic; music nonautographic". That is, the creator's *touch* is essential to the piece, while, for example, countless authentic copies of *Moby Dick* are in print, editions that Melville never saw, while the only authentic Van Gogh's were actually handled by the painter.

The other term,"plastic imagery," comes from the dramatic arts, specifically the film theory of V.I. Pudovkin (*Film Technique and Film Acting*), where he says that "plastic (visually expressive) material… [are] those forms and movements that shall most clearly and vividly express in images the whole content of [an] idea." The responsibility of a film or stage director or an actor is to create some outward movement or gesture, some plastic imagery, to convey an emotion or idea.

2. Beginning late in 1920, Picasso decisively abandoned the rigorous Cubism he had been pursuing (with periodic appreciations of Manet and Matisse). Thereafter a distinctly linear art appeared dependent as much on Ingres' wire line as citations from Greek vase painting and other antique classical sources. Conversely, his own painting, which beforehand often relied on patterns of flat color, became deeply modelled.

3. Although linoleum has been manufactured as a floor covering since the 1860s and has been used as a printing medium since the 1920s, few serious artists saw its potential. As a relief medium, gouges or lines made in the surface printed as "white" (the color of whatever parer is used) while the background, uncut, was inked. But both Mirô and Matisse executed linoleum cuts in 1938, and Picasso did some linocut work of note the next year, but not until the late 1940s did Picasso begin a series of color linocuts that blossomed into his masterpieces of the 1950s and 1960s, works of rare virtuosity, using a "reduction" printing technique that destroys the linoleum plate as the edition progresses so that neither changes nor additions are possible.

4. Core fellows are the recipients of an artist-in-residence grant from the University of Houston, which offers a one-year term fellowship in the arts renewable for a second year.

5. Meyer Guggenheim was one of five brothers whose fortunes were made in copper mining; his son, Solomon R. Guggenheim and his wife, Irene, were art collectors. Beginning in the 1920s they acquired French and Italian "primitives," French Barbizon School, and American 19th century landscape paintings, but, in the late 1920s (about the same time that the Museum of Modern Art opened in 1929), after meeting and falling under the influence of a German Baroness, Hilla von Ribay, the collection took a turn toward modern art, especially so-called,"non-objective" or abstract art. Guggenheim's collection soon included a prodigious 700+ works, and he decided not to donate them to any existing museum but to found one of his own, which opened in June 1939.

6. By 1951 the Guggenheim Museum collection numbered 1,400+ works, and a permanent home was now urgently sought in the building commissioned of Frank Lloyd Wright in the 1940s but not, until then, brought to completion; when Wright's building opened in 1959 the museum's collection numbered 2,500+ pieces.

7. This phrase may strike the reader as irreverent, but this series of work, beginning in 1966-67, is, in fact, called by Caro "Table Pieces." Small-scale works of steel, sometimes painted or polished, express their inherent size through one or more dangling elements that depend from the "main" mass.

8. From the mid-1960s Carl Andre began to present unorthodox sculptures that minimized the vertical (traditionally the "heroic") dimension and hugged the floor, effectively as carpets, often of contrasting square plates of metal alloys laid flat on the floor resembling checkerboards having only width and length without any operative verticality.

A little later, in the late 1960s and early 1970s, Richard Serra stacked or balanced heavy plates of (often Cor-ten) steel in ways that presumed the strength of the underlying floor or ground, making gravity an active player in his works.

9. In fact, while Mark Rothko (1903-1970)— like the rest of the New York School of Abstract Expressionists— never expected to make any money and suffered a long obscurity, by the time he was fifty-nine he was well-recognized, even famous, and in May 1962 was invited to a state dinner for the arts at the White House, not a sign of unrequited labor. Nevertheless, the pervasive sense of gloom associated with his solemn work and dour personality was capped by his suicide, which retrospectively tints his life with failure.

10. Barnett Newman's (1905-1970) first one-man show was a retrospective at Betty Parsons Gallery, January-February 1950. His first appearance in a significant group show had been at that same gallery only four years earlier.

11. Basil Bunting: "Poetry and music are both patterns of sound drawn on a background of time. That is their origin and their essence…if they lose touch altogether with the simplicity of the dance, with the motions of the human body and the sounds natural to man exerting himself, people will no longer feel them as music and poetry." ("The Art of Poetry", a lecture, 1970, quoted in Dale Reagan, "Basil Bunting: obiter dicta", in *Basil Bunting: Man and Poet*, Carroll F. Terrell ed., page 230.)

Earlier in the conversation I was referring to Bunting's notion of the possibility of beginning with the rhythms and cadences of dance, pure bodily exaltation, then proceeding to music which attaches a sequences of pitches to that pulse/cadence, then to words and, through their associations, eventually, to the plastic imagery of the visual arts. Not synesthesia but cladistics.

12. Toward the end of the 13th century a group of wandering AmerIndians arrived in the Valley of Mexico; this group claimed to have begun their journey from the semi-legendary town-on-an-island, Aztlán, and the descendants of these wanders called themselves Aztecs, the term now used to apply to the inhabitants of the Valley of Mexico from the 15th century onwards. In that valley, and in the middle of a lake, the Aztecs built their own capital, Tenochtitlán, which, when the Spanish beheld it, was probably the largest city on earth; it now lies beneath Mexico City. The "wall of skulls" represented in stone a reality, a frame that contained the heads of the innumerable victims of human sacrifice.

13. In 1872 the French art critic and collector Philippe Burty coined the word "Japonisme" to refer to the introduction into European consciousness of Japanese goods (mainly in the 19th century) and a taste for things Japanese, particularly in French art and design—although Japonisme had powerful effects in the graphic arts of America and in its architecture (Frank Lloyd Wright's career being mainly a commentary on Japonisme).

14. I heard this story from Louis Kaufman himself. An article about and interview with Annette Kaufman in the 11 June 2000 *Portland Oregonian* gives the full details, while a concise and scholarly version of these events can be found in: James E. Breslin, *Mark Rothko: A Biography* (Chicago: University of Chicago Press, 1993), p. 91. ("I took Marcus [Mark Rothko] to Milton [Avery]…and then he became a real fanatic on the work of Milton.")

15. Francis Picabia, one of the founders of surrealism, was born in 1879 and died in the same house in 1953 (26 rue Danielle-Cassanova in Paris) where his grandfather, a photographer, had befriended Daguerre and Nadar. Francis attended the Ecole des Beaux-Arts and the Ecole des Arts Décoratifs and before becoming a surrealist exhibited Impressionist-style paintings. He has the distinction of having made one of the greatest impressions in the early-twentieth-century Armory Show in New York, and thus acquainting, or disgusting, Americans with the idea of modern art.

16. Though developing from the discoveries of Guaguin, Cézanne and others, Henri Matisse's *Bonheur de Vie*—(*The Joy of Life*), 1905-06, the Barnes Foundation, Merion, Pennsylvania—is arguably the first work of 20th century modernism, the opening gun of what became modern art.

17. Born in Montevideo, Uruguay, but raised after the age of seventeen in his father's native Catalonia, where he was schooled, Joaquin Torres-García (1874-1949), though closely associated with the Dutch neo-plasticists, like Mondrian, and the Russian constructivists and suprematists, stands alone in citing sections of reality with any attempt to translate these into reductionist abstractions or universal synopses of experience. His influence upon modern art, particularly the New York School, has been immense. His sculptures are of wood.

18. Adolph Gottlieb's "pictograph" series of more than three hundred works, produced throughout he 1940s and early 1950s, aimed to create the sensation of confronting written texts without making any sign intelligible. A complete survey of the series' influence can be found in: Harry Rand, "Adolph Gottlieb in Context," *Arts Magazine*, February 1977.

19. Harry Rand, *Paul Manship* (Smithsonian Institution Press, 1989).

20. The painting by Jacques Louis David, *Oath of the Horatii*, 1784-85, hangs in the Louvre, Paris.

– Notes by Harry Rand

Looking is work and deserves

to be recorded as an activity.

To examine a work of art

is to attempt to bridge the

impossibly wide gulf between

souls.

What Matters

by Harry Rand

Making art carries responsibilities which have been acknowledged in, and have occasioned, a huge literature. We spectators concede our humility before the visual artist's accomplishments, inadvertently on our behalf. But, we viewers are not idle, limited to registering awe, confusion or disgust. Our looking carries responsibilities different from making art. The audience is far from passive, does not merely receive the visual arts which cannot, and do not transpire around or through us as music may invade our space and lives, passively, as we acquiesce to respond or not. Looking is work and deserves to be recorded as an activity.

To examine a work of art is to attempt to bridge the impossibly wide gulf between souls. Deep space holds nothing more immeasurably vast. Works of art come to us from elsewhere distant carrying messages, as in bottles thrown in desperation into the ocean. What is "meant" by a work is impossible to say, fully, finally. And the best art rewards us by never being complete, total, done. In time—which is life lived—things rise in estimation and fall away again: mountain ranges we approach and pass through in actual travel only to recall in some future. Things upon which we doted, people, foods or music, grow distant in temperament though before no excess sated us; we do not know how we fall out of love with things or humans. Uncommon vistas, sensations and arrangements arise and we are infatuated again, afresh finding some new corner of the soul ignited. That is the mark of successful art, or living. Novelty, and a stream of sensationalism, are hardly the point, are counter-productive, when the real issue is originality, a return to true things.

When art lives anew, transforming for us always, it is a monument in our lives; when played out against generations, a classic of civilization. Very little art can survive the circumstances in which it was made. When exhausted, when it fails, no longer among the pantheon of the best or favorite, art may not reach us at all or cease to. The dead-letter office of human desire failed. Mountains of yearning in artifacts unexamined, uncared for, unloved. These may be personal or society's discards. History travels light. It carries few bags into the future. The past, stuffed with every event and bit of data, is a sea anchor keeping history from moving forward, and memory can only accommodate so much baggage. Art has to return us to what matters and continues to matter.

The failure and the success of art have nothing to do with effort. The best and worst artist works as hard, as diligently, as hopefully and insecurely. The failure of sincere art is tragic, not merely sad. So we flat-footed meet each new work of art with hope for new love, usually dashed. The honest critic or viewer enters a gallery or studio hoping to find success, not failure. This attitude is not good-will but present gluttony and anticipated faith that we are not quite so mute and alone.

The art begins as foreign, speaking an unknown language perhaps recognizable in parts or recalling a half-remembered lullaby; it comes to us as from a far journey, as unfamiliar as gender to which we tentatively reach out approximating the unknown with the known, giving words to what is only estimated. (As in the ocean, where we are strangers, we mis-name the "sea wolf," "sea hare" and "sea cucumber" akin to what we know on land. There is some argument as to whether art is our true home—the theory that everybody is a genius at birth—or a window in the home through which we can see but not touch our native longing.) How much more distant to confront a room of art chosen not by style, medium, subject, political outlook or any other discursive affinity, but through the instrument of a personality unknown but for his own creations. We might feel twice-orphaned from the art. The labor of meeting the art "on its own terms" (whatever that might mean) is so much more enigmatic and demanding of self-awareness.

The art in this exhibition has not been chosen—as by a match-maker or other form of salesperson—because we will probably like it, but because somebody else already does, a person we do not know but whose words and works circulate in our world and may very well become our ambassadors to the future, as other ages are represented by furnishing our imagination with phrases and images whose authors have names. The past is outfitted by genius and anonymity.

Let us try to sidestep the curator's massive presence and look for ourselves (to find ourselves,

to do the looking undelegated, perhaps to find someone else) at
the exhibition's works. Albeit my insinuated words on this page,
read and sounding in your head, may provide an unwanted
basso ostinato, a redundant personality interrupting your
glimpses of the curator flitting between the works themselves.
This kibitzer will step out of the way, for awhile.

If we begin with **David Fulton**'s Untitled Neighborhood 1-5,
we might suppose he owes much to Eva Hesse, whose spirit per-
meates this show. Her piece, *One More Than One*, 1967, heralds
much of the floor-and-wall work we see presently; her *Repetition
Nineteen II*, 1968, seems the ancestor both of Thomas' multiples
and, in use of materials and form, Fulton's *Untitled Neighborhood
1-5*. This may not be obvious in Fulton's forms, necessarily, but can
be seen in Hesse's ground-breaking use of uncolored industrial materials which suggested that the
colors of these plastics—which discolor and fatigue under the effect of ultraviolet light's draining of
pigment—is not so much fugitive as mortal, and, hence, flesh-like. In Fulton's work light may be coming from within or without, or so it seems as these translucent vessels possess both a silhouette and
form; the record of incident light declares the surfaces it sweeps, adding up to form. Light also seems
to come from within the pellucid volumes like luminarias—the southwestern Hispanic Christmas
greetings that may line a snowy path with glowing boxes of light. (Not to make too much of this
now common custom, but Fulton could have seen this lovely southwestern practice when he was
awarded a 1989-91 Core Fellowship for the Visual Arts at the Glassell School of Art in Houston.)

Four years before Fulton's *Untitled Neighborhood 1-5*, **David McDonald** made the wall piece
94-8 stark and uncompromising in its arid surface. Its rectangular shape, size, and shallow space
belie that it is sculpture at all, and the eye is invited to enter a surface that seems like a painting in
form but which rebuffs scanning the putative picture plane. Scale and questions of aptness and
assumptions (presuppositions brought to the viewing which the artist up-ends or shares) are also at
the heart of a work like McDonald's *98-5* almost a miniature—if we could name the thing shown in
reduction. This sense of the contraction of an idea, its compression beyond its original status, under-
lies all symbolic communication, speech or graphic symbols. Something has to be made smaller than

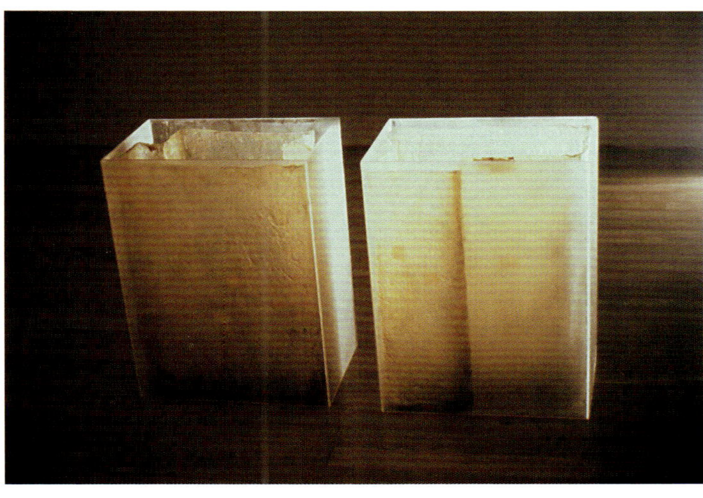

David Fulton
Untitled
1998
fiberglass, resin, plexiglass
18" x 15" x 10'

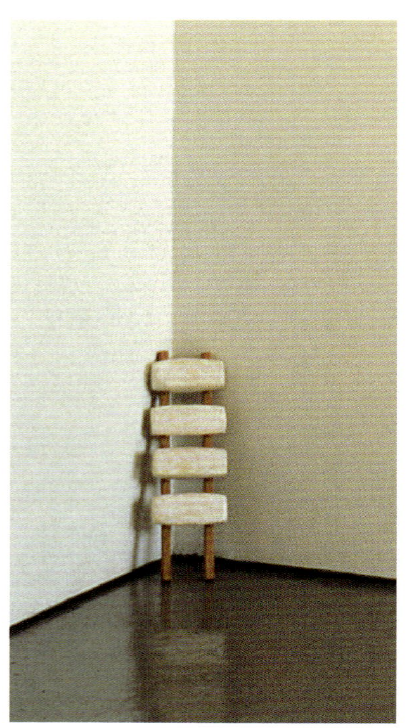

David McDonald
Untitled 95-47
1995
hydrocal, whiting putty
and wood
19' x 6" x 2"

it was, shorter or stripped of appurtenances in order to say something impossible in barter. Speech is not barter, something for something else, but more like commerce in which something is exchanged in a common unit, like money or words. This creation, the symbol, as the by-product of the idea of miniaturization, may be the single greatest human achievement and so, not surprisingly, is widespread in art.

This same sense motivated Joel Shapiro's dense little houses, a kind of "heroic" miniaturization. These buildings—defiant without preciousness—evidence a wrong-end-of-the-telescope Romanticism by which extreme diminution suggests sublimity. The spectator assumes the heady scale of a god. A formerly religious emotion was evoked for the secular purpose of presenting to the spectator the means by which such an emotion could be evoked—in the self-consciousness known as modernism. McDonald participates in this covenant fully. Another example, like his diminutive *93-8*—a work that laying low to the floor and hardly raising a silhouette might be construed as "heroic" or even sculptural in any traditional sense of that word's investment in molding space—seems reticent and invites the viewer to feel as if interrupting something subdued and quiet; which is another way of inviting the sense of time, of sequence, into an art that is stationary.

Something like this gesture toward miniaturization provided the substrate for Charles Simonds' miniature societies, in which the viewer assumes a tenderly curious god's-eye position of omnipotence. (If a sense of custodianship results, so much the better.) Representation is not at the heart of such references for McDonald. Indeed, Franz Kline's best monumental works imply an angle-of-vision that is level to the horizon or up, as do Adolph Gottlieb's *Blasts*—not sculptures but sculptural paintings. Paintings about nouns and verbs, actions and things, and their possible relationship.

McDonald's work plays out all sorts of references to recent modernist works (recent in the historical sense, not that contemporaneity of fashion, hysterically amnesiac). His *95-37*, and *95-47*, owe much to Donald Judd. The spectator must decipher what has been added to Judd's work in its repetitive rhythms that perhaps alter the non-redundant as sculptural in a way that sculpture had not previously admitted consideration. That is, in some ways Judd is the opposite of the minimalist and was extremely self-indulgent, in an astringent sort of way.

Diminutive art does not lessen its potential to be of consequence, and it does not necessarily traffic in minimalism—just look at the hundred-and-fifty years of small paintings of the Flemish Renaissance that each contain a world, uncramped, spacious, arresting and particular.

Richard Nonas' works invite classification as minimalist. If that is true, if that description feels comfortable and apt, then we must ask what is being reduced and focused, what eliminated, what concentrated. Subdued polychromed wood is remarkably even in its ambitions to hold some range of the visual field.

Nonas uses, in each of his four works in this exhibition, essentially the same materials and approach—which should not be surprising for work drawn from a single period. We are perhaps too accustomed to the marketing hype that parades new seasonal styles for whoring art to don, mistaking fashion's insatiable newness for art's originality. Novelty is of very little use in an art as circumscribed by Nonas' quiescence. No feigned angst. No dogs with pointy teeth prowling with mock menace beneath an impossible moon. No racial slurs or excrement. Nor for that matter, feigned gestures toward cool technology. You will find nothing fashioable or shocking in Nonas' wood pieces but he does maintain a remarkable concentration of attention, and the viewer is rewarded for the artist's narrowly defined, methodical, and unwobbling progress. Here we see the first requirement of great art everywhere and at all times: ethical rigor. Whatever the superficial appearance of the subject or its treatment—agitated or tranquil—whatever the theme (or without a named subject), whatever the medium, that ethical precision is art's foundation and salvation. It is, besides the pure pleasure art affords, its only use. Art presents the arena within which ethical failure is played out beyond the consequence of worldly concern. Consult the poems of Gilbert Sorrentino on this.

Mia Westerlund Roosen is represented by a single work, an experiment that seems in retrospect sheer artistic intelligence. *Pulse*, 1997, combines the verticality of traditional free-standing sculpture with a stubbornly repeating rhythm she seems to favor, all set into a necessary relationship with the adjacent wall. Necessary because structurally indispensable to the piece which, set against any wall, becomes "site specific" as it weds vertical and horizontal elements of present architecture, which it presupposes.

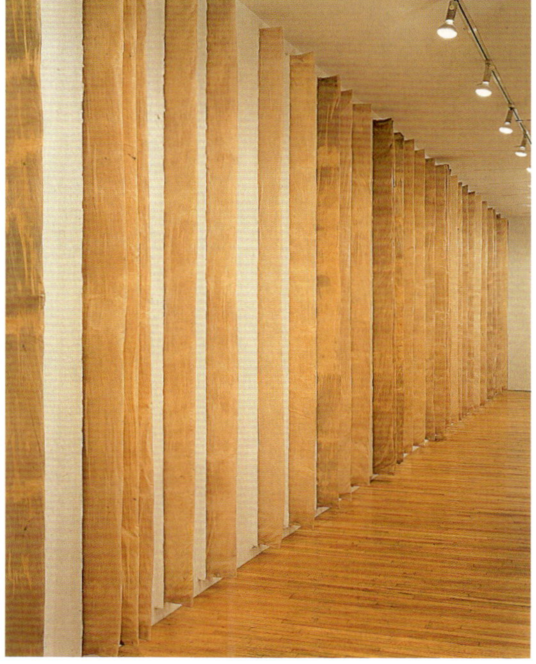

Mia Westerlund Roosen
Pulse
1997
cotton and resin
12 1/2' x 69'

Although in *Pulse*, the wall does predominate, it does not govern her work to the exclusion of other considerations.

Likewise, **John Beech**'s *Double Trough*, 1997, stipulates some relationship to an established, built architectural plane. Supine, red and brilliant yellow, the patterns with which the piece is painted neither complement the work's massing by emphasizing volume, nor in any obvious way does the painting seem (like camouflage) to negate the work's slight, hollowed-out bulk. Beech sets up an absorbing syncopation between the forms and the two-color scheme—the intense red, subordinate to the yellow, flitting across the surface with the flicker of a tired neon sign given new life.

Another floor piece, **John Duff**'s *Linked Rings*, 1999, is among the show's more complex works formally. It relies neither on modular repetition nor the model of artists like Hesse or Andre so much as Robert Smithson and even some of the nearly-forgotten shaped-canvas artists of the 1960s and 70s. Working with steel, plaster and cement, Duff provides something quite substantial—another facet to the idea of "matter" in the exhibition's title. Yet, despite its serious construction, the preponderance of *Linked Rings'* area and bulk is the empty space embraced at its core. The work modulates between absence and presence, mass and emptiness, the spiral's attraction and repulsion readable inward or outward, the flat floor plane upon which it rests and the space above through which we see down to it and into which it minimally rises—not as minimalism but as the most efficient and least obtrusive gesture upward.

Working out of a similar set of assumptions and a closely related artistic tradition that relies upon Judd, Andre and others, **Barry Goldberg** is represented by a garland of five works including *Pure*, 1992, and *Within Without*, 1995. The scale of these sculptures distinguishes them as among the larger in the exhibition. Yet, the vocabulary of repeated elements stacked vertically recalls other such compositions; only the relationship between floor and ceiling is unique.

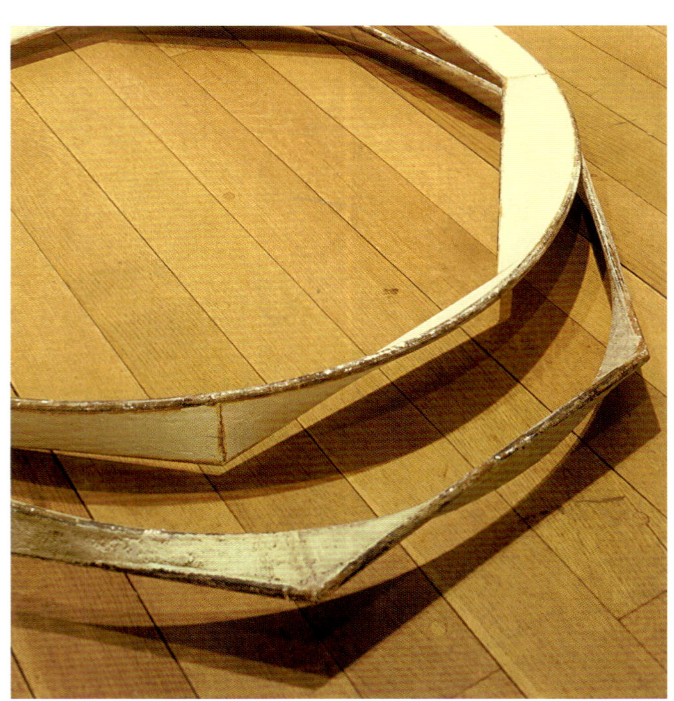

John Duff
Linked Rings (detail)
1999
steel, plaster and cement
diameter: 51 ¹/₂"

The spindly components of *Within Without* frame space like drawing in air, but this construction is palpable. (As Basil Bunting would have it in his 24th Ode: "Here was glass-clear architecture.") The sum of this lacy fabrication concentrates attention upon the opaque box floating mid-way in air. Like a reliquary, something precious is held aloft. Inevitably the hieratic comes into play as attention focuses back upon this density amid light air and lighter construction, brawny as bird's nest. We become aware of our own mass, our own strength, next to such fragility, and what is modernism if not the presentation of its own assumptions before the spectator as part of the art, and mass and light are the food and wine of sculpture. That is the sacred meal Goldberg has prepared for the spectator.

Jonathan Thomas is represented by one untitled piece from 1999, or an aggregate, or a choir, depending on what one sees as the irreducible unit of art. His *Fragment*, 1999, unfurls in a room of forty-five sculptural columns made of pulp, paper, and acrylic polymer on wood. That so many elements can be made disparate and forced to reconcile, or at least attune, to a single over-riding personality is not a new idea, only in need of re-invention within the history of modern art.

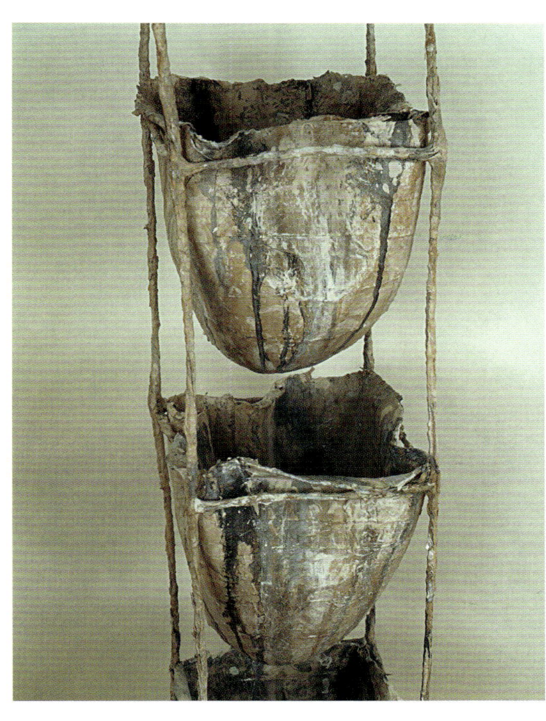

Barry Goldberg
Pure (detail)
1992
plaster, fabric and steel
93" x 11 ½" x 10 ¾"

Whole armies of sculpture bedeck the old cathedrals of Europe, and no one decries their resolution into a larger whole. They do not submerge or lose anything. The modern idea of the sacred individual had no place in these sculptured assemblies and we do not know the artists who made them. The cherished anonymity of these Gothic pieces is broken by close examination; we have our favorites that we pick out for singular attention, but each piece exists only as part of the ensemble. Likewise, there are delicious tunes in serious music, evanescent—a clarinet solo, perhaps, that fleetingly wafts through a symphony, its poignancy heightened because it departs—so the rest of the music can move along. Not every player is always a soloist. Soliciting this ethos of team-work (that survives in sports, in industry and the industry of film-making, theater, and orchestral music), Thomas injects multiplicity where we have become comfortable with

Jonathan Thomas
Fragment (detail)
1999
pulp, paper on wood, acrylic polymer
Forty five columns:
fifteen - 6' x 6" x 3"
fifteen - 4' x 6" x 3"
fifteen - 26" x 6" x 3"

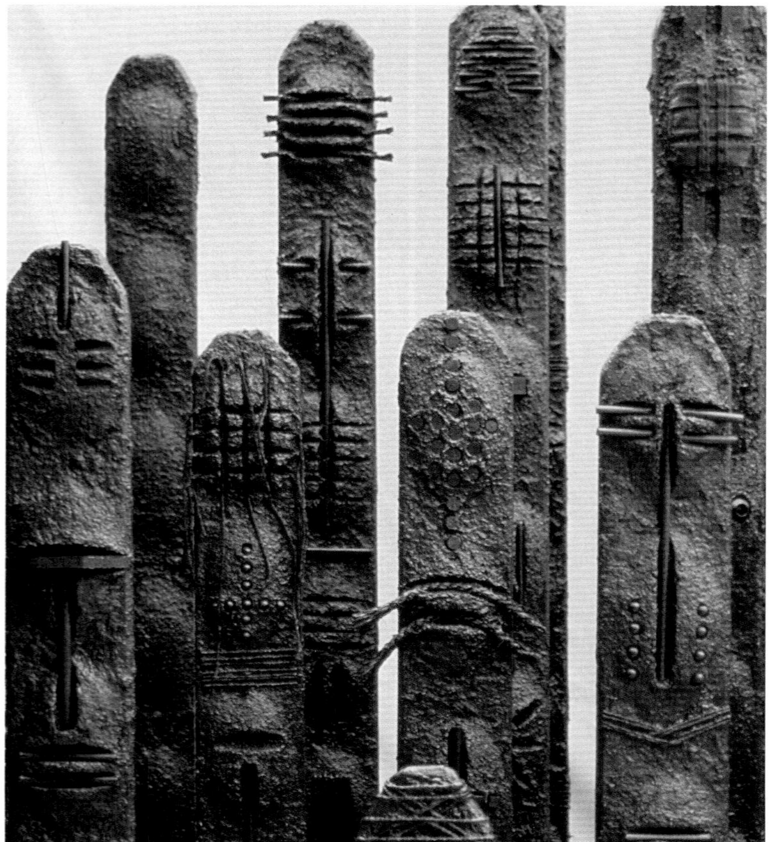

the assertive identity of the artist's surrogate: the individual piece, specific as the ego if not distinctive. We largely assume, in the modern (and post-modern) world, that the artwork is the representative of the artist, whatever the degree of sincerity in the presentation; the artwork stands alone, the lonely challenger up-holding the artist's tenets. Instead, Thomas gives us a squadron of forms.

The urban crowd is not an ensemble, submerging in restless alienation what a choir or freely associated body jettisons. Uneasy detachment, nervous self-consciousness and longing—the lack of these distinguish the choir from the crowd. The singular name and past and identity all mingle in the mob. The crowd is an unhappy or happy aggregate, while it is entirely unclear if Thomas's work is composed of units any more than the sound of an orchestra can readily be reduced by eliminating "excess" elements. There is a moment when the parts are famously exceeded by the whole.

Thomas's work manifests the spirit of collecting, the compiling of things found, but not usually made by the seeker himself. He both looks and finds. Finding is important to art, and from the root of the word that gives French its *trouver* (to find) old Provençal supplies *trovar*, from which we get troubadour, the finders of form, in fact, of troves. Thomas willingly places himself amid this pre-modern heritage of finding and arranging.

Paul Whiting has contributed three untitled works from the same year. They are as close as anything in this show to the Romantic sculptural tradition of the discrete unit, independent of its encircling space and spurning the volumetric surround it shares with the spectator. (Here one thinks of that huge heritage and fraternity including Michelangelo, Rodin's Balzac, Julio Gonzalez, even Calder and the New York School sculptors.) Whiting, more than many in this show, is willing to make evident his stake in fashioning space. Then coloring it. Form and color are separable and not inherent in his materials. Nor are we meant to feel they are somehow, mutually intrinsic. (This was a lesson taught by Kenneth Noland and the early Frank Stella, but it is a lesson worth re-learning, or, as Ezra Pound noted, "Art is news that stays news.") His materials, though apt and lovingly handled, are less essential to his task than many others in this show, and Paul Whiting's work might easily have been made of painted steel, not building board and chalk.

Also, though his range of forms in a single year flirts with the support of the floor, Whiting's historic reference to sculpture feels most comfortable and successful as a form, however complex, pitched in air.

Though we are not obligated to, memory elides such a show into a common sensation, a single perception combining all the features we care to remember. Every player contributes to a symphony, but the instrumentalists start out with that intention of merging—not the visual artist whose demand is "look at me!" In a show, personalities elide and ricochet, and what was made in aching solitude ends up a comparative. There are as many combinations as chemical reactions, but the whole exhibition is the reactive vessel, the retort and alembic. Works blur into a general sensation of "the show." A piece may stand out for this-or-that quality, but there is also, inevitably, if damnably, the parallel sensation of "the show" as if it possessed a life not of its constituent works.

The Exhibition becomes a new entity with its own colonizing power to overlay a language of souvenir perceptions, since we cannot take the works with us. This sensation only heightens with time, with distance from the event. Only now, when show and catalogue are embryonic, is the circumstance fresh.

What to make of these apparently disparate observations—mine and the artists'. Do they add up to anything at all or are we faced with an impenetrable randomness? On the one hand, it is easy to over-determine, to assume a higher meaning within some pattern and thereby, insisting, find such. On the other hand, all of this work was gathered by a single personality; the works might share some commonality. There is an old Talmudic story on this point (as long as we acknowledge that most Talmudic stories are indeterminately old): Two men set out from a

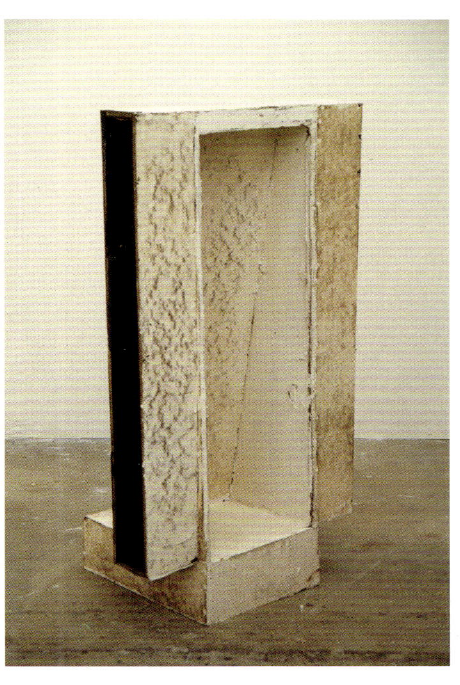

Paul Whiting
Untitled
1998
building board, plaster
48" x 26" x 16"

kingdom far-distant from the empire's center. Their ambition is to glimpse the emperor. After crossing oceans, deserts, mountains and having many dangerous adventures they arrive at the glittering imperial city where, making their way through the bustling mazy streets, they at last come to the breathtaking palace, at which point one of them gives up. We will never find the emperor in such a huge hive! I am going home. But, says his companion, even if we do not ever see the emperor by wandering the corridors of his palace and seeing with what splendid goods he surrounds himself, we will gain some insight into his majesty. The point in its original context was that study of law leads to righteousness and some inkling of absolute good (the sacred) and ultimate meaning (the holy). In our context, by wandering the literal and figurative corridors of this exhibition and seeing with our own eyes the splendidly select objects Edward Albee has chosen, we may gain some insight into his temperament.

The works are all spare. Nothing in them seems ornamental; no form is added to an underlying form. They are conspicuously lean. In that sense they may be, as an aggregate, thought of as minimalist. Not because they are, as a group, a series of gaunt forms, but the work tends to be minimal because most of it represents the least means with which they could be presented, could come into being. (Of course, there are in the show exceptions to this generalization.) Also, quite clearly none of the forms are representational. They are not in any obvious way "symbolic." And because they are not symbolic in a literal way, they do not engage themselves within any literary or anecdotal narrative. This is relatively easy to confirm with a thought experiment: one cannot readily imagine that the pieces were any different in a fictional moment before we espied them; nothing within the works' own continuance indicates the passage of time interior to the pieces. They are not stories or about stories or chronological time, although the sequences of their construction (a slight narrative, native to the visual arts), is also usually suppressed in these pieces—the only nod to craft.

The works do not celebrate how they were made. Skill is not on display. Indeed, there is a kind of tacit falsity: craft suppresses any sense of "truth of materials." We are not intended to ponder, or be arrested by, or to deeply consider how these works were made, only that they are. They are, then, images as much as things, which may explain the frequently encountered sensibility in this show so akin to the aesthetic of ancient icon makers. Where a sense of materials does surface it is not the natural condition of things—unique substances' irreducible identities known by color texture and weight. (Wood has a feel, we know it rough or smooth, and its many smells; the coolness of metal and its polish or lacerating edges are known for their comforting strength of threatening sharpness; the porosity of ceramic; the rhythm of fabric woven, or the blur of felt; etc.—materials have distinct quality, and for a century it was the highest aim of crafts and some arts to work from these truths toward something expressive. Very little of that sensibility is visible here.) Artificially worn surfaces, or the use of found objects, contribute a kind of ruggedness, and that knock-about "history" is all we know of these forms' putative past. They come on the stage of our consciousness redolent of the past they survived, or seemed to. That is, as personages with character that endured travail, they seem to matter.

— **Harry Rand**
Curator of Cultural History
Smithsonian Institution
Washington, DC

That is, as personages

with character

that endured travail,

they seem to matter.

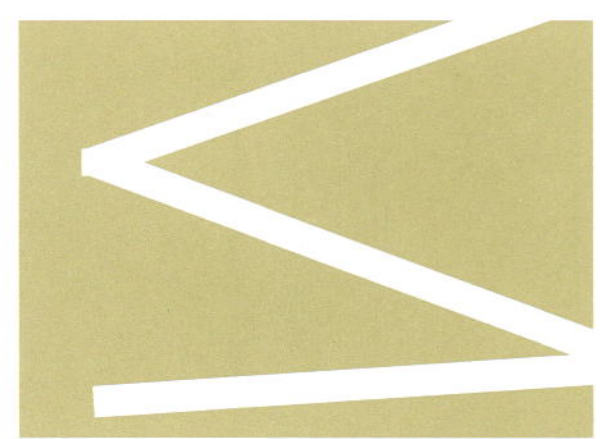

John Beech

John Beech received his BA from the University of California,
Berkeley, in 1986. Beech's work had been shown in several
exhibitions, including a recent solo show at the Petra Bungert
Projects, Brussells, Belgium, and will be seen in an upcoming
exhibition in November at the Stark Gallery, New York City.
His work is in various private and public collections, including the
Laguna Art Museum, California, and the San Francisco Museum
of Modern Art. In 1999 Beech received the Pollack-Krasner Award.

For *From Idea to Matter*, Beech will exhibit several new and
recent sculptural works utilizing such materials as plywood,
metal pipes, rubber and primer.

John Beech lives in Brooklyn, New York

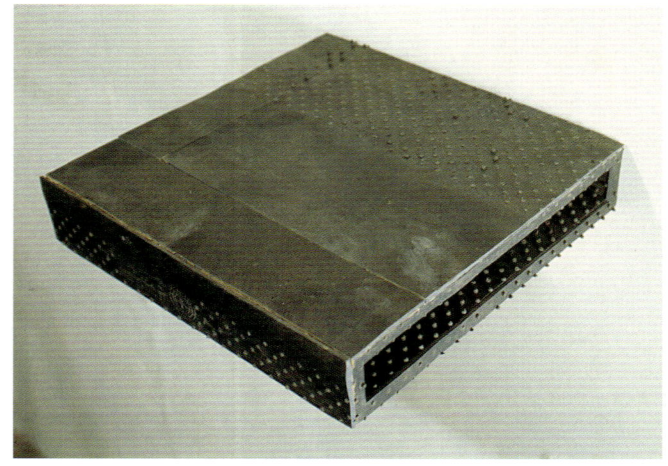

Left: *Car - Mat Sleeve #24*
1996
rubber, plywood, adhesive
2" x 10" x 10"

Right: *Double Trough*
1997
plywood, plasterweld
118" x 26" x 6"

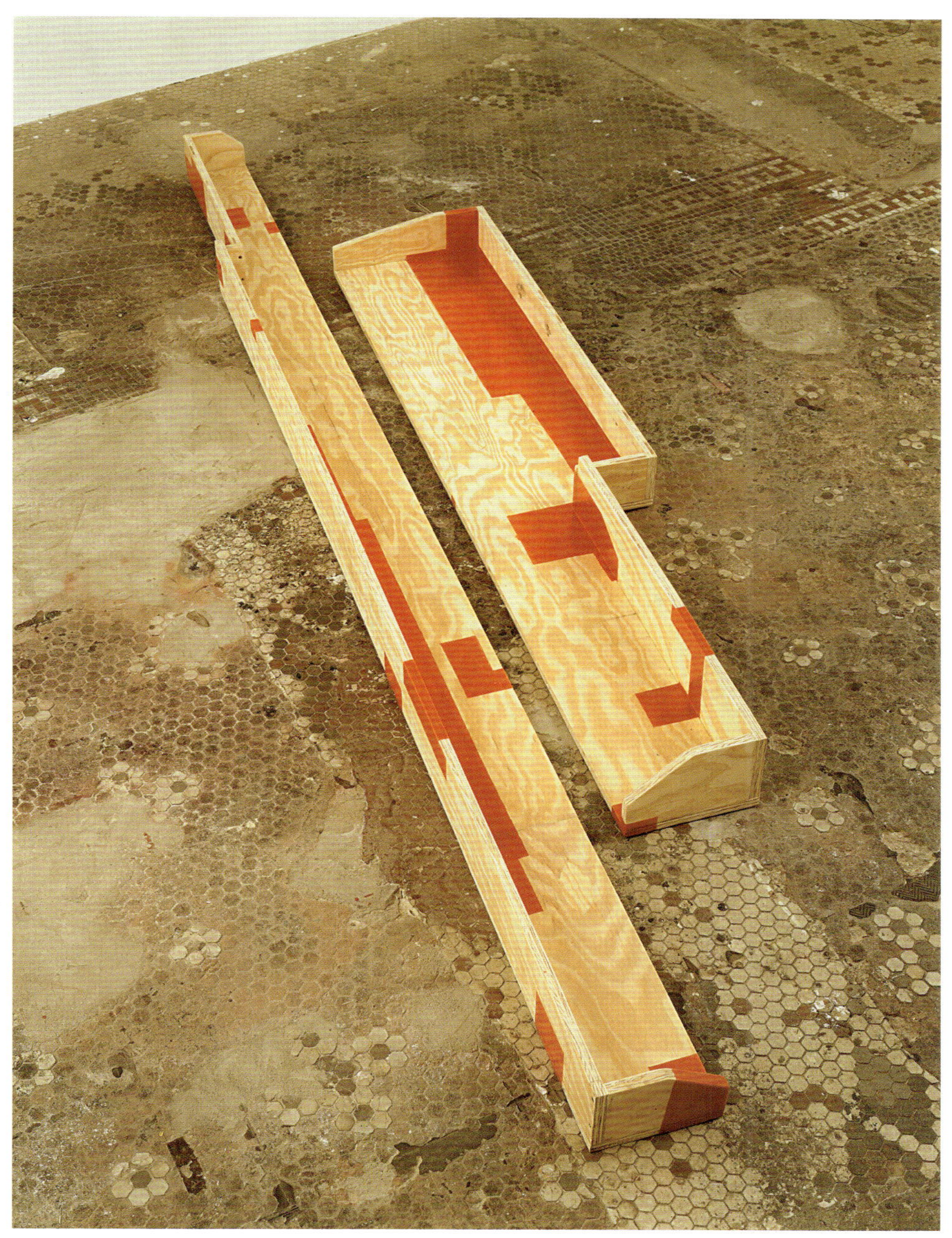

John Duff

John Duff received his BFA from the San Francisco Art Institute.
Duff's sculptural works have been shown in numerous
one-person and group exhibitions in New York, California,
Holland and Germany. He will also be in an upcoming
joint exhibition at Knoedler and Company and the Baumgartner
Gallery in New York in 2001. His work is in various public
collections, such as the Museum of Contemporary Art, California,
and The Museum of Modern Art, New York.

For *From Idea to Matter*, Duff will exhibit a new steel and plaster,
work titled *Cosa Mentale*.

John Duff lives in New York

Right: *Linked Rings*
1999
steel, plaster and cement
diameter: 51 ½"

Below: *Cosa Mentale*
1999-00
steel and plaster
62" x 37" x 46"

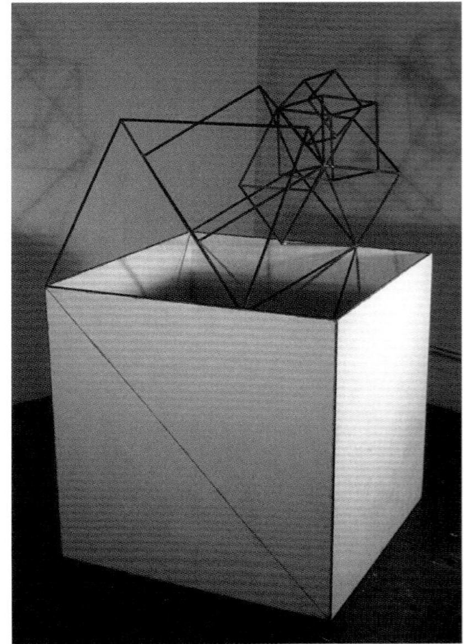

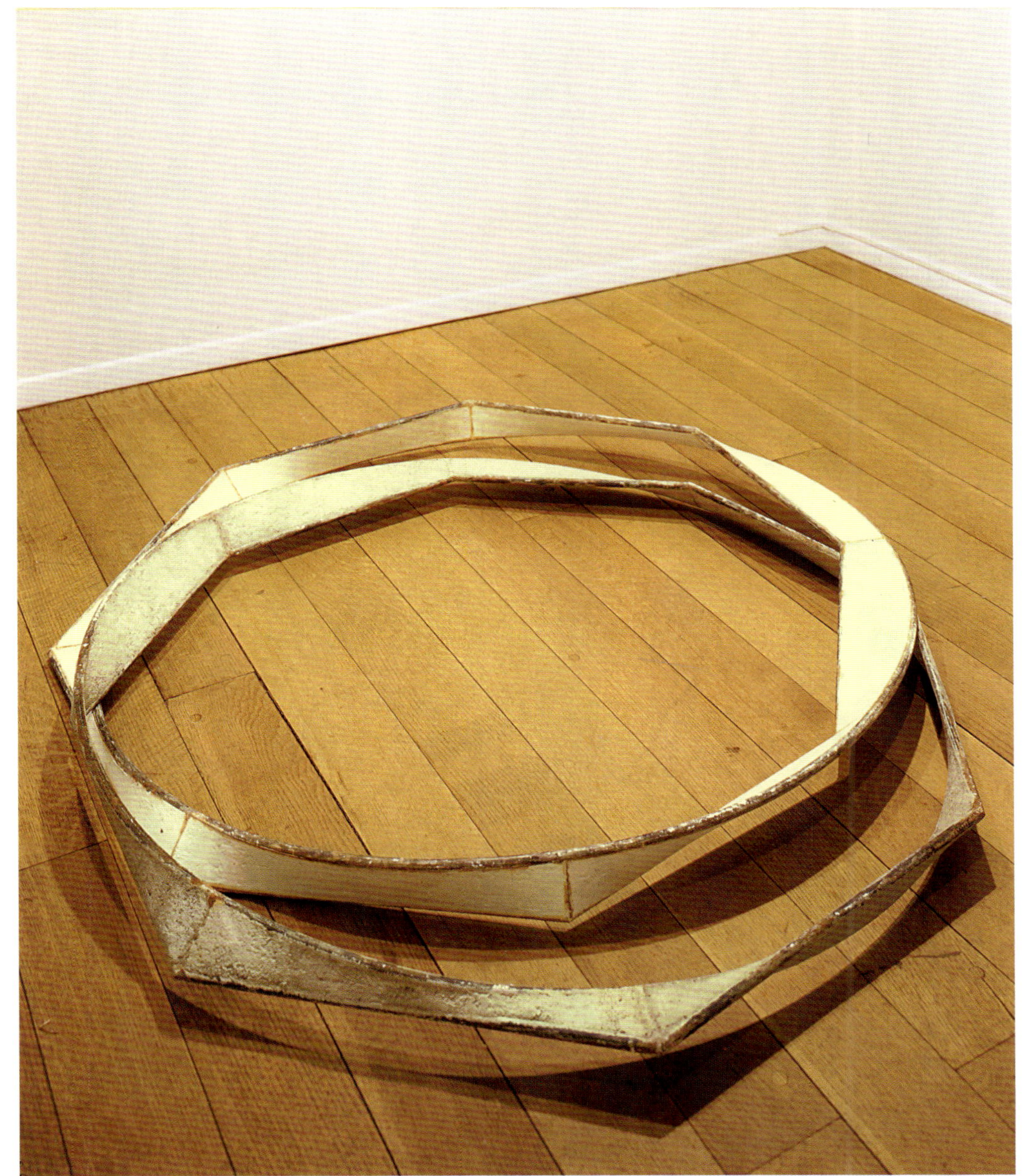

Images courtesy of the artist and Knoedler and Company, New York, NY

David Fulton

David Fulton received his BFA in painting from the Tyler School of Art, Temple University, in 1988. Fulton was the recipient of the Core Fellowship for the Visual Arts from the Glassell School of Art, Museum of Fine Arts in Houston, Texas, from 1989 to 1991. Fulton's work has been seen in numerous group exhibitions in the United States, including *New Realities, From Collage to Digital* at the Museum of Fine Arts, Houston. He has also had solo exhibitions at the New Gallery and the Contemporary Arts Museum in Houston, Texas.

For *From Idea to Matter*, Fulton will exhibit *Untitled (Neighborhood)1-5*, a sculptural work utilizing fiberglass, resin and plexiglass.

David Fulton lives in Houston

Untitled
1998
fiberglass, resin
and plexiglass
18" x 15" x 10'

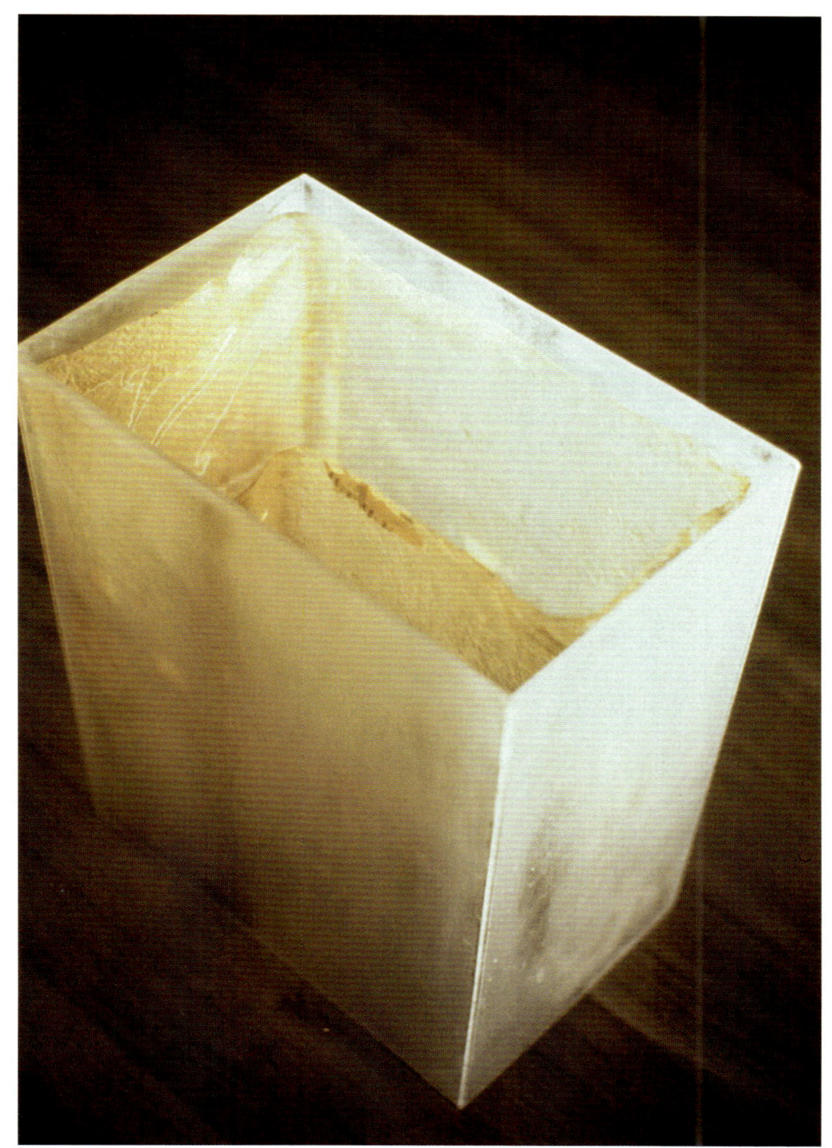

Barry Goldberg

Barry Goldberg received his BFA from the Cooper Union in
New York in 1981. Goldberg's work has been in numerous
solo and juried group exhibitions, including shows at the
Viridian Gallery, New York, Pleiades Gallery, New York, P.S.1.,
Brooklyn, and the Lidewij Edelkoort Gallery, Paris. He
has also received several grants and awards, including two
Pollack-Krasner Foundation Grants.

For *From Idea to Matter*, Goldberg will exhibit several
recent works utilizing materials such as plaster,
steel, fabric, wax, paper, ink and organic materials.

Barry Goldberg lives in Brooklyn, New York.

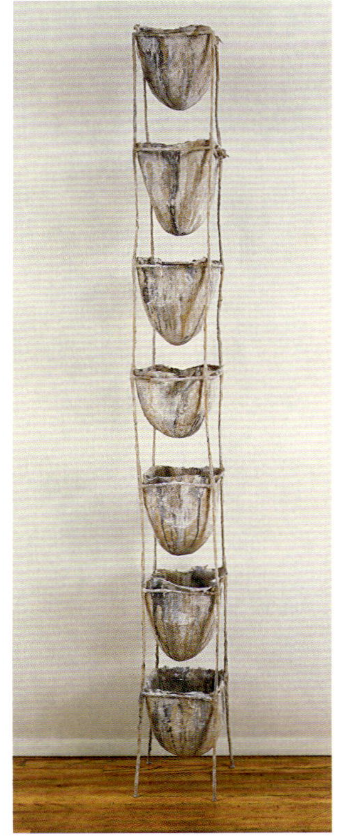

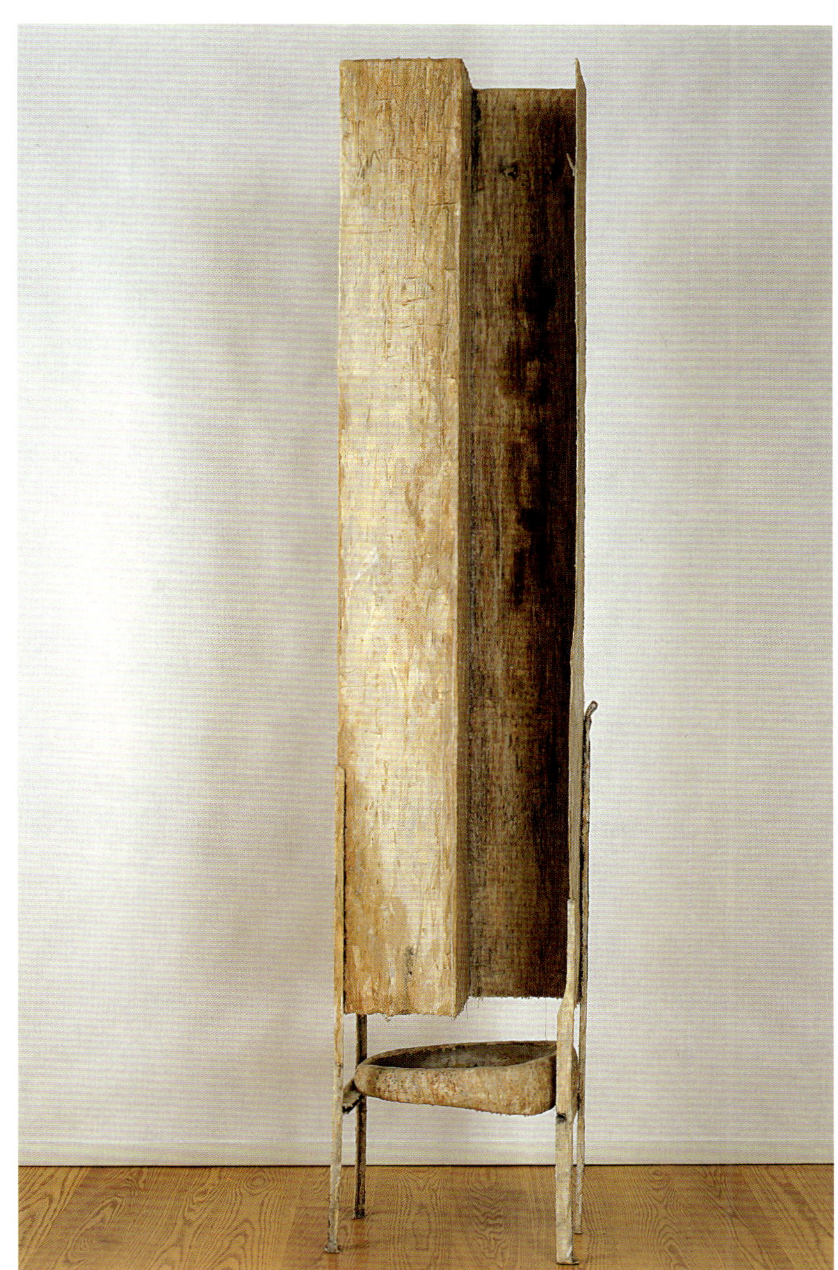

Left: *Pure*
1992
plaster, fabric and steel
93" x 11 $^1/_2$" x 10 $^3/_4$"

Right:
Wax Works-Pure No. 5
1992
plaster, fabric and steel
108" x 10 $^1/_2$" x 10 $^1/_2$"

David McDonald

David McDonald received his BS from Boston University in 1980.
In 1988, McDonald completed the Diploma and 5th year Program
from the School of the Museum of Fine Arts, Boston. He
received his MFA from the California Institute of the Arts,
Valencia, in 1992. McDonald's wall and floor works have been
in several solo and group exhibitions in California, including
In the Details at the Irvine Fine Arts Center and *Plastered* at
Shoshana Wayne Gallery. He has also exhibited in New York,
Arizona, the Netherlands, and Korea.

For *From Idea to Matter*, McDonald will exhibit several untitled
sculptural works.

David McDonald lives in Topanga, California

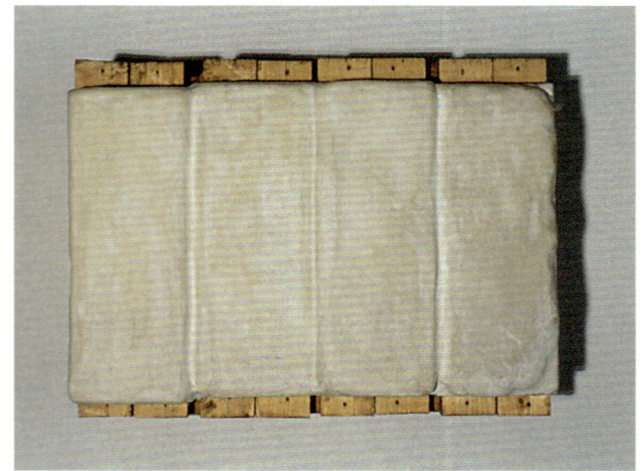

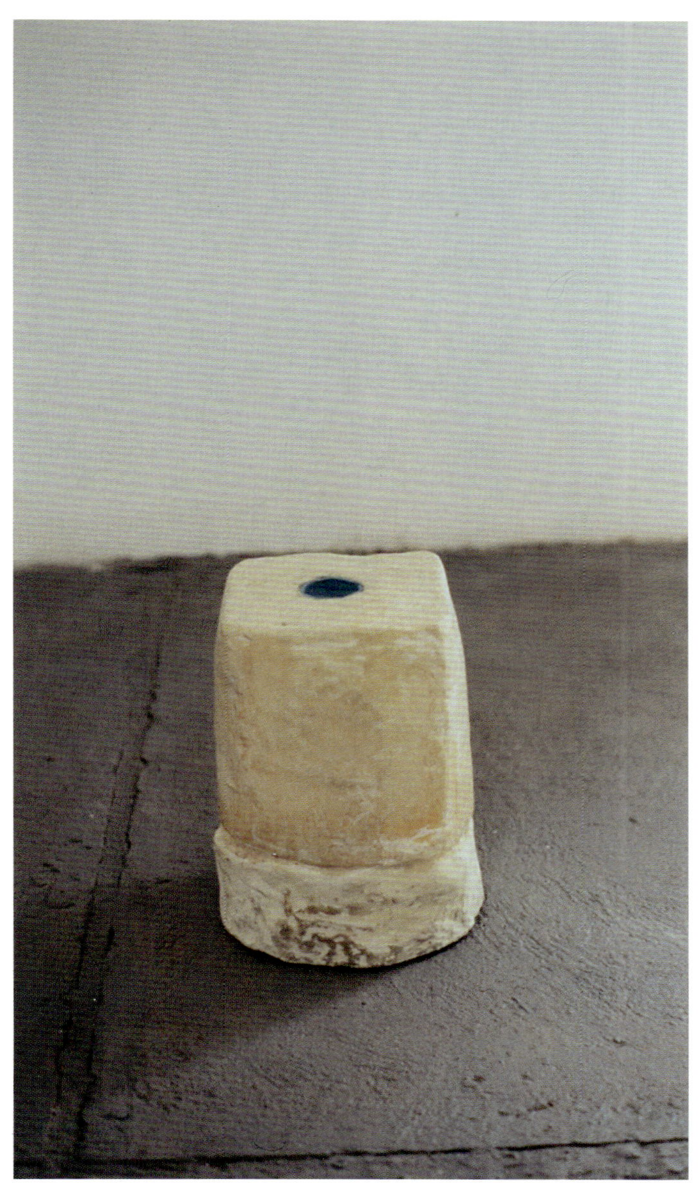

Richard Nonas

Richard Nonas was educated at the University of Michigan,
Layfatte College, Columbia University, and the University of
North Carolina. Nonas has exhibited his sculpture nationally and
internationally and recently has shown at the Musée d'art
Modern et Contemporain in Geneva, Switzerland, and completed
permanent installations of his sculpture in Austria, France
and Sweden. His work is included in the collections of museums
and other public institutions throughout the world. Nonas
has received awards from the Guggenheim Foundation,
the National Endowment for the Arts and the New York State
Council for the Arts.

For *From Idea to Matter*, Nonas will exhibit several of his
wood sculptures.

Richard Nonas lives in New York

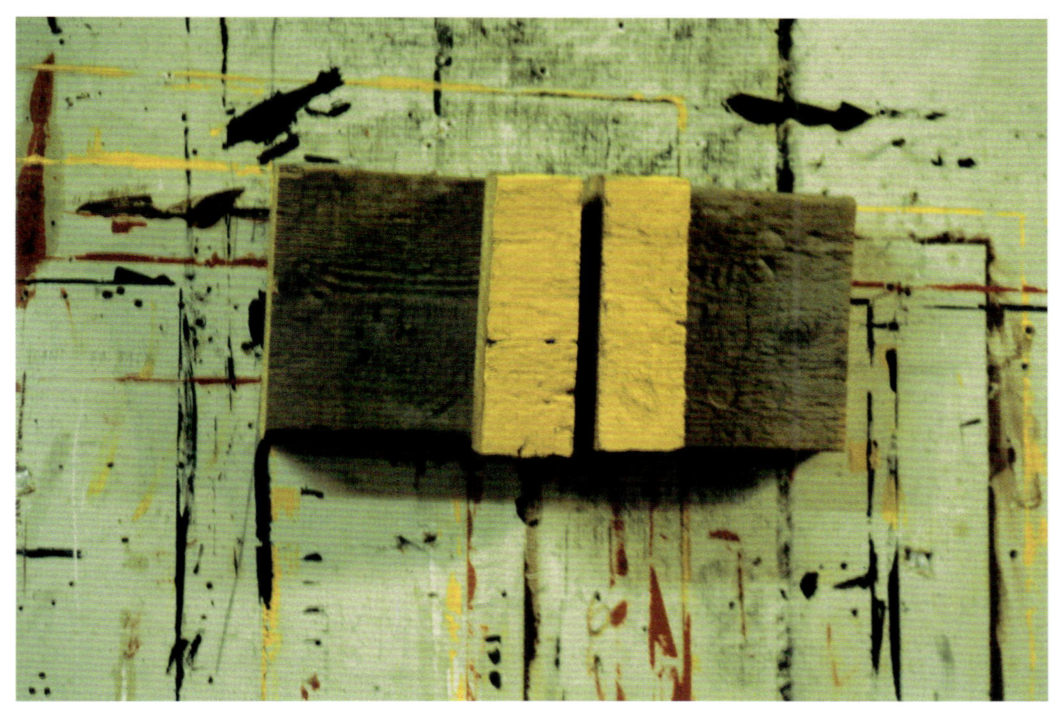

Untitled
1985
oil paint on wood
18 ¹/₂" x 8 ¹/₂" x 3 ³/₄"

Jonathan Thomas

Jonathan Thomas received his BA in Art History and his BSc in
Mathematics from McMaster University in Canada. He completed
graduate studies in Art History at the University of Toronto,
Canada. Thomas' work has shown in several exhibitions, including
solo shows at New Gallery, Houston, Jack Tilton Gallery, New York,
and the Wadworth Atheneum in Hartford,Connecticut.
His work has also been in group exhibitions at the Hillwood Art
Museum, in Brookvile, NY, the Rosa Esman Gallery in New York
and several Chicago Art Fair Group Shows.

For Idea to Matter, Thomas will show his multi-piece work,
Fragment, 1999, featuring forty-five sculptural columns made of
pulp, paper, and acrylic polymer on wood.

Jonathan Thomas lives in New York

Fragment
1999
pulp, paper on wood
and acrylic polymer
Forty five columns:
fifteen - 6 ′ x 6″ x 3″
fifteen - 4′ x 6″ x 3″
fifteen - 26″ x 6″ x 3″

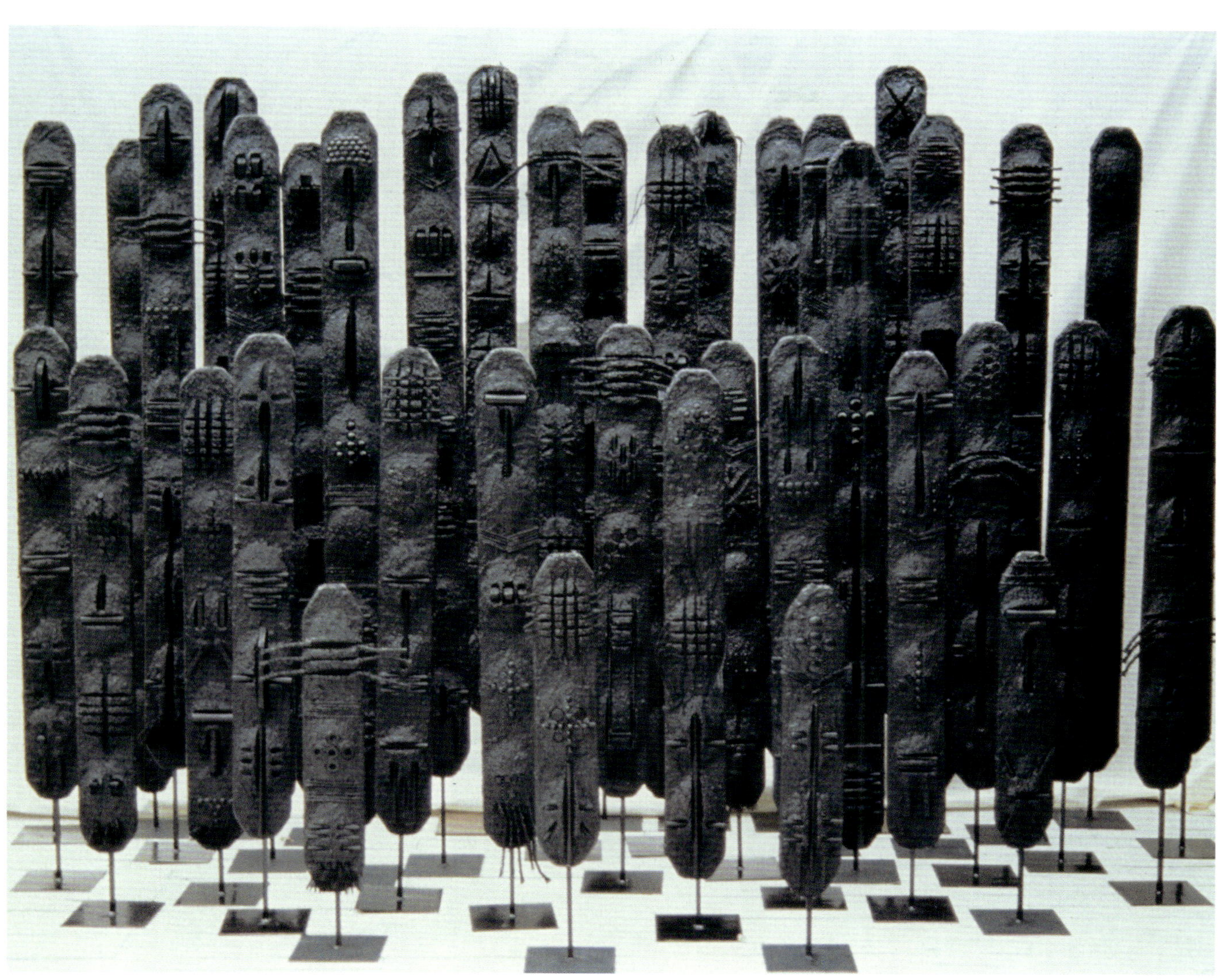

Mia Westerlund Roosen

Mia Westerlund Roosen's work had been seen in numerous solo
exhibitions, including a recent show at the Shoshana Wayne
Gallery in Santa Monica, California. Her work was also included in
group exhibitions at the Montclair Art Museum, New Jersey, and
the International Kunsthalle, Drewen bei Kyritz, Germany. She
has been the recipient of numerous grants and awards, including
a Fulbright Fellowship. Her work is in the public collections of the
Metropolitan Museum of Art and Yale Art Gallery.

For *From Idea to Matter*, Westerlund Roosen will be reconfiguring
a major site-specific sculptural work, *Pulse*,1997.

Mia Westerlund Roosen lives in Buskirk, New York

Pulse
1997
cotton and resin
12 ^{1}/$_2$' x 69'

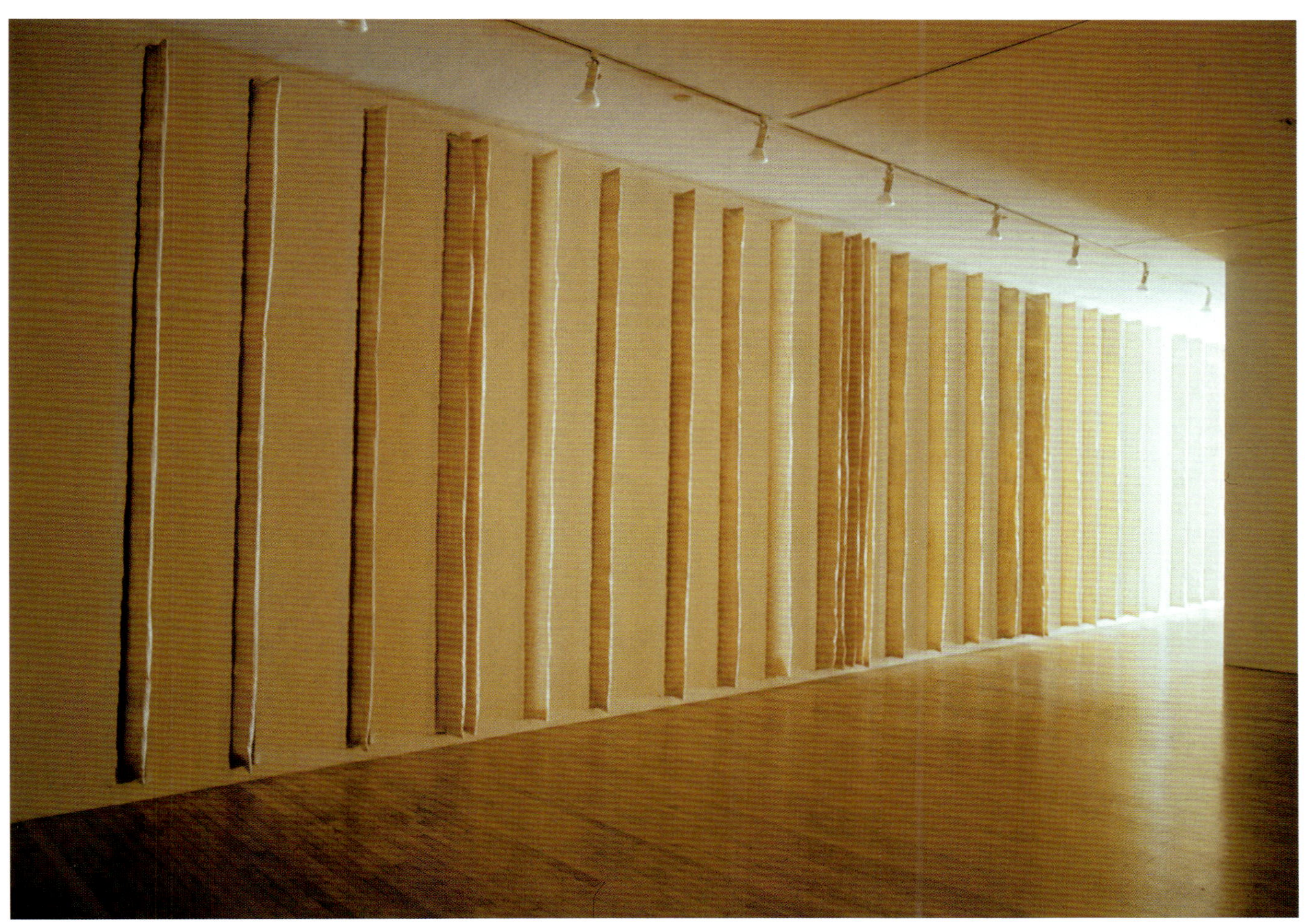

Image courtesy of the artist and Lennon, Weinberg, Inc., New York, NY.

Paul Whiting

Paul Whiting received his BFA from the Cooper Union in New York in 1986 and received his MFA from the School of Visual Arts in New York in 1997. Whiting has shown in exhibitions in Houston and New York. He has been a participant in the Core Artist in Residency Program from 1997 to 1999 and was included in the Core exhibition at the Museum of Fine Arts, Houston. Whiting was the recipient of the Eliza Prize, Core Program, Museum of Fine Arts, Houston, in 1998 and the Rhodes Award from the School of Visual Arts in 1997.

For *From Idea to Matter*, he will exhibit several floor sculptures utilizing building board and plaster.

Paul Whiting lives in New York

Untitled
1998
building board,
latex paint
51" x 22" x 74"

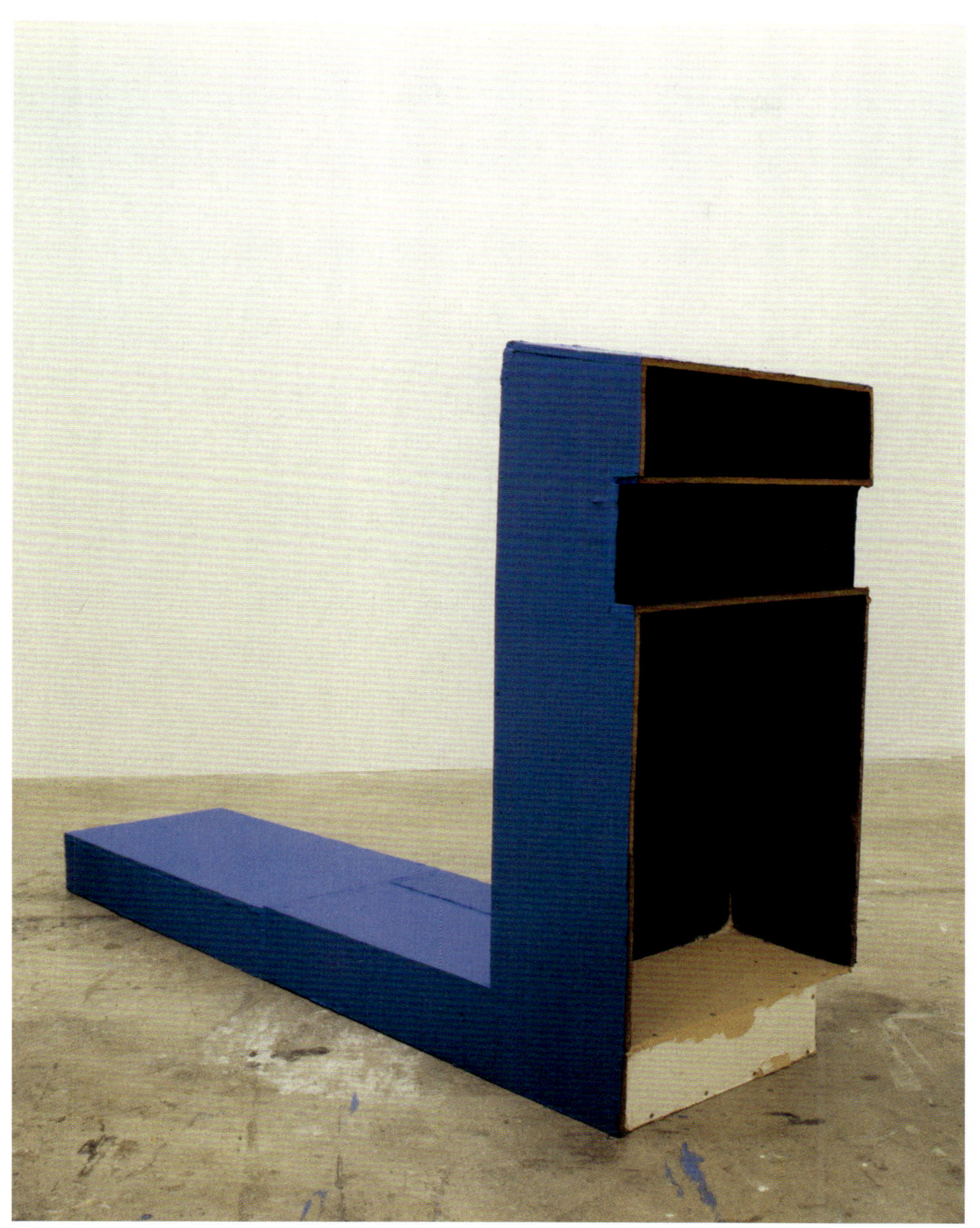

from Idea to Matter

Checklist

John Beech
Far-I
1999
rubber pipe, handles,
primer and steel brackets
91 $^1/_2$" x 8 $^1/_2$" x 7 $^1/_4$"

John Beech
Double Trough
1997
plywood, plasterweld
118" x 26" x 6"

John Beech
Minott
1999
plastic pipe, handles
and primer
102" x 9" x 6 $^1/_2$"

John Beech
Car - Mat Sleeve #24
1996
rubber, plywood
and adhesive
2" x 10" x 10"

John Beech
Green Block
2000
plywood, metal pipe
and enamel
7 $^1/_2$" x 7 $^1/_2$" x 7 $^1/_2$"

John Duff
Linked Rings
1999
steel, plaster and cement
diameter: 51 $^1/_2$"

John Duff
Two Triangles
1977
steel
47" x 96" x $^1/_2$"

John Duff
Cosa Mentale
1999-00
steel and plaster
62" x 37" x 46"

David Fulton
Untitled (Neighborhood), 1-5
1998
fiberglass, resin and plexiglass
18" x 15" x 10'

Barry Goldberg
Pure
1992
plaster, fabric and steel
93" x 11 $^1/_2$" x 10 $^3/_4$"

Barry Goldberg
Pure (No. 2)
1992
plaster, fabric and steel
108" x 10 $^1/_2$" x 10 $^1/_2$"

Barry Goldberg
Wax Works- Pure No. 5
1995
plaster, fabric, steel and wax
103" x 21 $^1/_2$" x 13"

Barry Goldberg
Within Without
1995
plaster, steel, ink, paper
and wax
105 $^3/_4$" x 33 $^1/_2$" x 27 $^1/_2$ "

Barry Goldberg
Untitled (No. 118)
1997
plaster, organic matter,
rubber, steel paper, ink
and wood
29 $^1/_2$" x 18 $^1/_2$ " x 23 $^3/_4$ "

David McDonald
Untitled 94-8
1994
whiting, emulsion, glue
and putty on stained wood
7" x 12" x 4"

David McDonald
Untitled 98-5
1998
hydrocal, wood, putty,
paint and emulsion
4" x 18" x 8"

David McDonald
Untitled 95-37
1995
hydrocal, whiting, putty
and emulsion
eleven units - 4" x 5" x 4" each

David McDonald
Untitled 95-47
1995
hydrocal, whiting, putty
and wood
19" x 6" x 2"

David McDonald
Untitled 93-8
1993
hydrocal, whiting, emulsion
and wood
5" x 12" x 12"

David McDonald
Untitled 98-11
1998
hydrocal, putty, paint,
emulsion and varnish
11" x 8" x 8"

Richard Nonas
Untitled
1971
wood
119" x 113" x 2 ¹/₂"

Richard Nonas
Untitled
1985
oil paint on wood
18 ¹/₂" x 8 ¹/₂" x 3 ³/₄"

Richard Nonas
Untitled
1983
wood
16" x 16" x 5 ³/₄"

Richard Nonas
Untitled
1991
wood
29 ¹/₄" x 9 ³/₄" x 3"

Richard Nonas
Untitled
1999
wood
38 ¹/₂" x 11 ¹/₄" x 3"

Jonathan Thomas
Fragment
1999
pulp, paper on wood,
and acrylic polymer
Forty five columns:
fifteen - 6' x 6" x 3"
fifteen - 4' x 6" x 3"
fifteen - 26" x 6" x 3"

Mia Westerlund Roosen
Pulse
1997
cotton and resin
12 ¹/₂' x 17' x 14"

Paul Whiting
Untitled
1998
building board and caulk
8" x 42" x 14"

Paul Whiting
Untitled
1998
building board and latex paint
51" x 22" x 74v

Paul Whiting
Untitled
1998
building board and plaster
48" x 26" x 16"

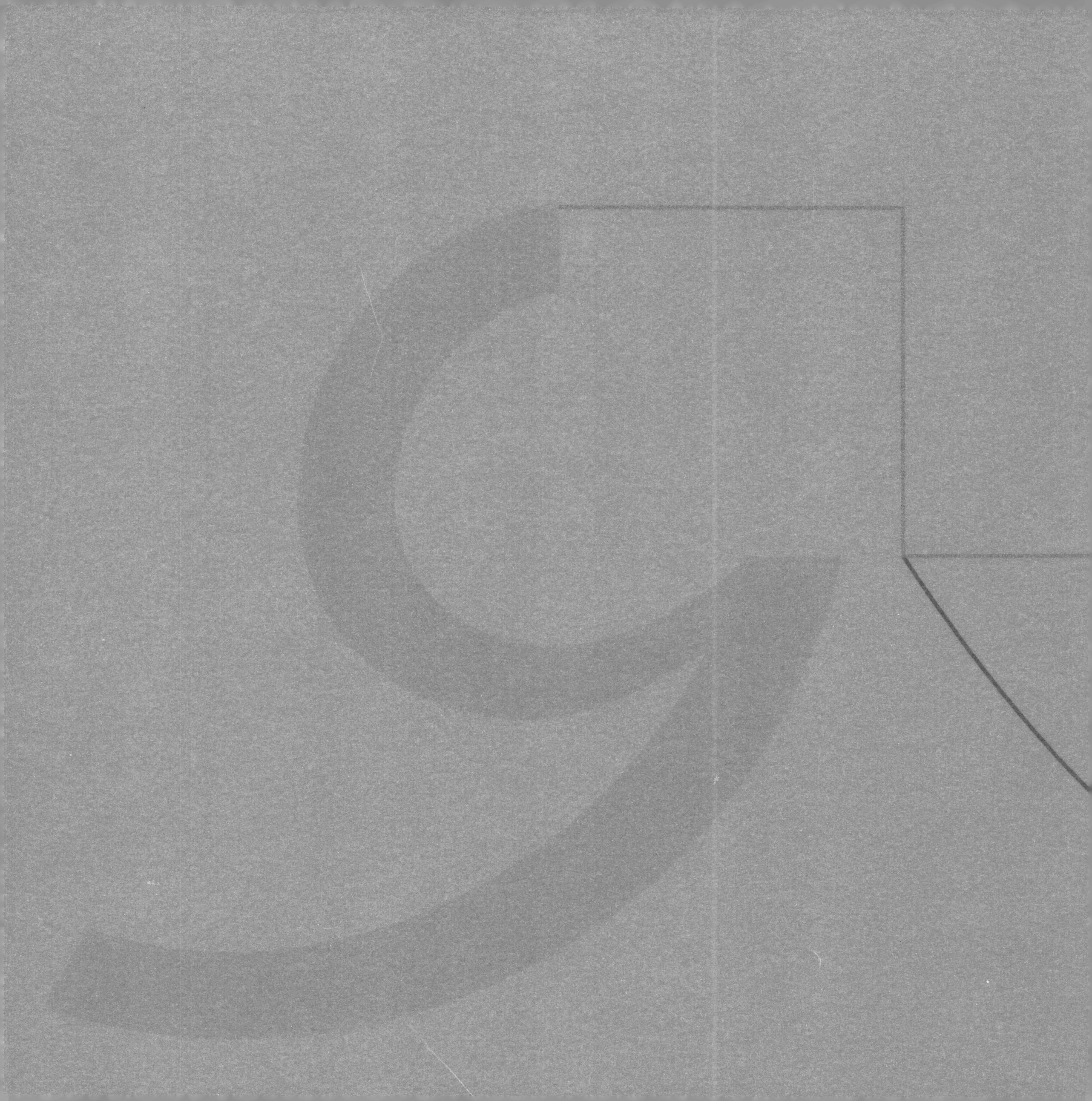